My one Contribution to
CHESS

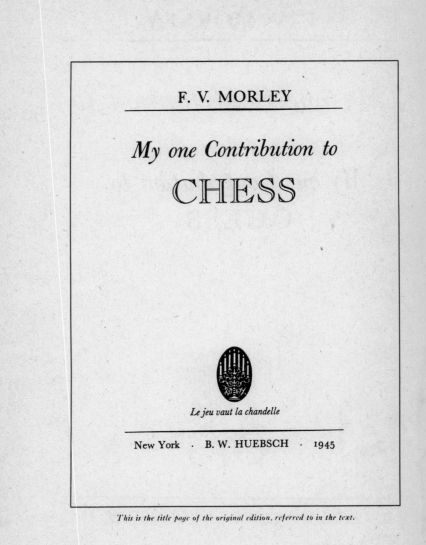

F. V. MORLEY

My one Contribution to

CHESS

Le jeu vaut la chandelle

New York · B. W. HUEBSCH · 1945

This is the title page of the original edition, referred to in the text.

F. V. MORLEY

My one Contribution to

CHESS

GEORGE W. STEWART, PUBLISHER, INC.
New York   1946

It is a pleasure to us to take over the further publication of this work.

George Woodbridge Stewart

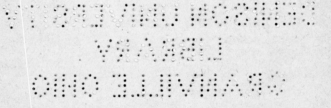

Advertisement

BOOK PUBLISHING is sometimes pompously referred to as a profession; sometimes — in mistaken condescension — as a trade. Those who get the most out of the vocation, who elevate it and are elevated by it, find book publishing a happy and inspiring way of life. But publishing must take second place to writing, for what would publishers do without authors?

It is a day to rejoice the cockles of a publisher's heart when he encounters a manuscript with which he feels at one. Those moments of satisfaction are not necessarily evoked only by masterpieces for the ages or by such as promise large gain; more often they have their origin in a modest work which combines head and heart in rare balance. Likelier than not it will be a composition for the few rather than for the million.

These words may serve to explain to readers who for twenty years have not seen the name and candlestick which appear on the title-page why I gladly exhume, for the purposes of this essay, an identity so long abandoned.

— B. W. HUEBSCH.

CONTENTS

My One Contribution to Chess

1

Put the papers on the sundial. . . .
Conan Doyle, *The Five Orange Pips*

SURELY no publisher has ever been bedevilled by his author in the way in which I have been bedevilled by my author-brother Christopher to publish these remarks.

I'm afraid Christopher is a very innocent fellow. It is probable that he has never read THE LOGIC OF SCIENCE, a translation of *The Posterior Analytics of Aristotle,* with Notes and an Introduction by Edward Poste, M.A., published at Oxford in the year MDCCCL by a publishing house now defunct. The first sentence of Mr. Poste's Preface reads as follows: " There is pretty general agreement among those who have devoted any attention to Logic, that the Logical works of Aristotle would repay the labour of a perusal." I have no doubt of that (I am a little shaken, though, by the demise of that publishing house) but what bothers me is that there is no general agreement that I know of, among those who have devoted any attention to chess, which would call for any work of mine on the subject. Do you suppose that Christopher is in some way preparing to protect himself? — either directly in the spirit of Job (O that mine adversary had written a book) or more deviously to defend the brochure published under his name in or about the year 1927, with the title " My One Contribution to Seventeenth Century Scholarship."

Alas, the one contribution which Christopher urges me to put on the sundial is not just an addition to scholarship, but is in a more serious realm. Possibly it has something to do with postwar communication; with communication between individuals who have not shared the same experience; with the problem, in the Pauline sense, of conversation.

The contribution is no less than a new realm of chess, to be achieved by a modern chessboard.

What title have I to promote the suggestion? No title at all, except that I enjoy games in general and chess in particular, although I am not good at it. In that last fact is my only excuse. There is no lack of books on chess by experts. Good books too, I hasten to add, since the publishing house I belong to distributes some of them. It can scarcely do harm to add to these important books a stripling whose object, though in such a serious realm, is mere adventure. It might even give pleasure. What did the gentleman say to Don Quixote? — " I am more inclinable to read books that are profane than those of devotion, if they be such as yield an innocent amusement, and are agreeable for their style, and surprising for their invention. . . ." I shall trust I am among such gentlemen here, and so have done with apology.

Yet before I attempt to advocate a different chess-board, let me at once make clear that I expect no change whatever in the familiar chessmen. No change in the number of pieces, no change in their characteristic moves, no change in any of the established rules and conventions of the game. So far as the chessmen are concerned it is in every way the same chess. I am not quite certain how to construe the motto of the State in which I am now residing. The motto is: *Quis transtulit, sustinet.* If I understand it correctly, I am being faithful to the intention. In this particular pursuit of happiness I am pinning less expectation on the perfectibility of chessmen than I am upon improvement in the field of play. The proposed change is simply in the board. I count on there being the same old combatants, but I would set them on a wider field of combat.

Not to make any more mystery, here is the suggestion. Figure 1 shows the old:

FIGURE 1. Ancient

[3]

Figure 2 shows the new

FIGURE 2. Modern

The sole difference in these two diagrams is the addition of a new corridor to each side of the ancient battleground. That simple difference is not without a meaning. It alters a war of fixed positions to a war of greater movement. Any chess player who glances at Figure 2 will notice new possibilities, new openings, new combinations, new thoughts let loose in new directions.

2

What apparence soever there be in novelty, I do not easily
change, for feare I should lose by the bargaine. . . .

Montaigne, *An Apologie of Raymond Sebond*

WHY should one wish to make such a change, or any
change, in chess?

It is agreed, there's no compulsion. None whatever. You don't have to contemplate the slightest
shadow of variableness if variety doesn't appeal to
you. Supposing, for example, that all old chess-
boards like Figure 1 were in some way confiscated,
and there was nothing on which to play chess but
boards like Figure 2, you could still agree with your
opponent to cover up or disregard the corridors and
play the ancient game to your heart's content. It is
the very essence of a game that players can agree to
play in any way they choose, and, unmolested and
unhampered, go on playing the game which pleases
them both, with mutual satisfaction.

But suppose the game no longer pleases them
both?

One thing which might alter the game is, of course,
the romantic temperament. "Come!" cried old
Omar. "Let us drink, and break into new patterns
the tedious roof of heaven!" Some other top-flight
fellows in chess have expressed themselves that way.

[5]

Edward Lasker remarks: " I believe that we remain interested in a game only as long as it mystifies us. As soon as we know all about it play becomes mechanical and boresome." And the great Capablanca, feeling that chess had become stereotyped, endorsed the suggestion of a board ten squares wide, with four extra chessmen on each side.

I made no claim to be an expert; I make no claim to be a romantic. Change merely for the sake of change, I grew out of long ago. All I ask is that the pattern of things should in itself be not too bad, and in its effects not so intolerable as to stifle individual experiment. The individual experiment, in its turn, being subject to the spirit of the game.

The pattern of the ancient chessboard has not tired me, and I myself am in no position to contend that chess on the ancient board is stereotyped. For me it isn't. For me each new game is a new adventure. How can I claim to know all about it, when I am aware that there are as many as 197299 ways of playing the first four moves in chess, and nearly 72000 different positions at the end of those first four moves (two on each side) of which 16556 arise when the players move pawns only?* So many possibilities afford to such as me an irresistible temptation. At the very beginning of a game I am the centipede who lay distracted in the ditch, considering how to run. Or to change the metaphor, the ancient board is to me

* W. W. Rouse Ball, *Mathematical Recreations and Essays*, Macmillan, 1911, Fifth Edition, p. 110, gives the references for these calculations.

[6]

still an unbelievably rich pasture, and that is partly why I am so often the bullock who, while he speculates as to which blade of grass is preferable, is slain by the opposing tiger who is out to kill.

The top-flight fellows have a right to say the ancient game no longer mystifies them. I have made it plain that I am one of the ruminants, and don't know all about it, and am not tired of it for that reason. For me the old square chessboard is rich in surprises. Then what *is* my complaint, and why should I be making what my children call " personal remarks "?

Though I speak as an underdog at chess, my complaint seems to coincide with the complaint of the romantic experts. By an opposite route, I arrive at the same restlessness. Chess on the ancient board can never be stereotyped for such as me, yet no one can deny that the game has been studied in a way that is both world-wide and intensive to such an extent that the serious player (the fellow who reads the books we publish and practises his reading) does enjoy an overpowering edge over the gallant amateur. And in a game that's played for fun shouldn't both parties rebel against any set-up which invariably rewards the ant and invariably slays the grasshopper? Should any sport (or art or science for that matter) invariably repulse the gallant amateur, or force him to become professional? Isn't that to be resented from below, as much as from above? Yet isn't that what happens when a game becomes over-studied?

The portentous number of opening moves just

mentioned turns out, of course, to be illusory. The possible openings are not all equally effective. How do you know that? Well, your unaided ingenuity will tell you something, but you needn't rely on yourself, for it has all been studied, and it is all available as inherited knowledge. The number of moves is further cut down because in any given contest Black's moves and White's are interdependent. White's beginning to a large extent controls, even dominates, Black's reply. On that, the available knowledge is immense. It might almost be better for a talented beginner not to bother about playing an actual game, but instead apply himself to lonely, isolated study of the books. The openings, the replies, the successful continuations have been so frequently recorded, analyzed, commented on (with variations noted), and so many post-mortems have been indulged in for so many years, that one would think there could be considerable tension in the mind of a newspaperman whether chess should be reported on the sports' page or on the page devoted to obituaries.

Yet, from the point of view which I've acknowledged, isn't my complaint a little emotional? Haven't I been getting unduly excited? All that knowledge about chess is surely innocuous. You don't have to go in for it if you don't want to. You don't have to play by the book. You can have a friendly game without being stifled by learning. The remark about the ant and the grasshopper overstates the situation. In the Book of Proverbs from which that metaphor is taken, there are other little people mentioned, who though they are weak yet manage to put up a game.

"The conies are but a feeble folk, yet make they their houses in the rocks. . . . The spider taketh hold with her hands, and is in kings' palaces. . . ."

If that is the rebuttal to my argument, I haven't made the situation at all clear. Perhaps that personal question — why should I be interested in any change in chess — calls for a personal illustration.

3

But no longer at ease here, in the old dispensation . . .
T. S. Eliot, *Journey of the Magi*

MY FATHER, Frank Morley, born of Quaker stock in the East Anglian town of Woodbridge, Suffolk, was a natural chess player. My brother Christopher has written about Woodbridge, and, notably in the novel called *Thorofare,* has given an amusing picture, if a little fanciful, of the family background. Christopher gives the impression that Woodbridge was sleepy. But Christopher's earliest recollections date only from the eighteen-nineties, and my father was born in 1860. I don't think sleepy is the right word for Woodbridge as it was in my father's boyhood. On the record, the rather unusual number of notable men associated with the little town betokens a tradition there of intellectual curiosity. The days of George Crabbe and of Charles Lamb's visits to Bernard Barton, the Quaker poet, were of course before my father's time, but Edward FitzGerald (his *Rubaiyat of Omar Khayyam* was written at Woodbridge and published the year before my father was born) was a familiar figure in the town, with his green Irish cape, flowered satin waistcoat, an old pair of slippers on his feet, and, if the East wind was blow-ing, a silk handkerchief tied over his hat and under his chin. Thackeray and Spedding, and more frequently Carlyle and the Tennysons, were visitors who came to stay with FitzGerald at Woodbridge, and they would purchase their newspapers at John Loder's bookshop, and their tobacco either at the " Bull " or at the " Crown," and then, along with Fitz, make their " discreet journeys in uneventful directions " on foot or on the river Deben in Fitz's boat, the *Scandal*.* On the part of the townsfolk, in so far as they were differentiated from the Gentry, there was considerable awareness of what was going on in the world. John Loder at the bookshop and Mr. Redstone at the Seckford Library, warmly discussed the motions of contemporary literature. These were close friends of the family, as was Barlow Wood, the painter, and a lively fellow. Also the

* The *Scandal* (a small schooner, 15 tons,) was named, Fitz said, for the " main staple " of Woodbridge. The boats wore out, but he went on naming them *Scandal II, Scandal III*, . . . As for the tobacco, Alfred Tennyson, while walking in the garden of Fitz's house, Little Grange, before breakfast, made one of the worst puns ever made in Woodbridge or about smoking, when he excused himself by referring to " the earliest pipe of half-awakened bards." † I don't know why I should mention it, except that as to the genius of Woodbridge punning plays as great a part as kenning does in Anglo-Saxon literature.

† Christopher swears " It was EFG who looked out of the window of Little Grange before breakfast, saw Tennyson smoking, and made that horrific (and memorable) pun." I will admit that is one school of thought. The truth is it takes two people to make a pun, and if it is memorable each claims it from, or blames it on, the other. I speak from personal knowledge, not of Tennyson and FitzGerald, but of my brothers Christopher and Felix, of Woodbridge, and of puns.

[11]

Seckford Grammar School was then at its prime, and the Mechanics' Institute was promoting the excitements going on in science with lectures from Huxley and other worthies (among them I believe was William Kingdon Clifford). To us American children of a later generation on summer visits to the ancient town (the visits always seemed to coincide with the annual Woodbridge Flower Show) the heavy ozone of the Deben estuary and the gorgeous surfeit of sausage rolls and batter puddings made sleepiness compulsive. It is my recollection that Christopher and Felix, like two Fat Boys out of *Pickwick,* were practically always in a swound. But Aunt Bertha did not make those sausage rolls and batter puddings until she had nephews, and as I review the evidence it is clear to me that in my father's boyhood the inhabitants of Woodbridge were fairly wide awake. Trade was not awake. Business was stagnant — at least it was in the family china shop in the Thorofare. But fiscal prosperity and intellectual curiosity don't always fall or rise together.

What I started out to say is that my father was a natural chess player, and that while he was a boy he achieved a local reputation for the game. When he was not more than ten or twelve his father encouraged him to make tours from Woodbridge to such centers as Ipswich, Debenham, and Wickham Market to play against the best that they could muster. The summer before he died, he mentioned the great battle he once had with the butcher in Debenham. Of more importance than the butcher, Sir G. B. Airy, the Astronomer Royal, retired, about the year 1870, to live at Playford, a couple of miles from Wood-bridge. Airy, though he was beginning to get on in years, had by no means lost his unusual gift for exact and elaborate computation.* By all accounts the hard-headed old gentleman and the Quaker trades-man's son had a very good time playing chess to-gether. When my father's father died, in 1878, and the death-rattle of the china trade was heard in the town, it was Airy who insisted that though the others of the family might at once go to work, my father should prepare himself to go on from school to Cam-bridge.

You never know what may happen when you start to play chess. It may lead to problems beyond the game, within and without the family, beyond the bor-ders of prognostication. Airy's plan that my father should go to Cambridge was hard to manage. The available scholarships were extremely meager. Worse than that, such a plan was not in the family tradition. It must be remembered that in the 1870's non-conformists had only recently been allowed to take University degrees. Even at Cambridge the general manner of University life was not sympa-thetic to small-town Quaker people. Those preju-dices were not one-sided. I strongly suspect that when my father won a scholarship to King's College, it sent (on account of the *King's*) a thrill of horror through his tight-lipped Quaker mother and the more rigid of his sisters (I am thinking of Aunt Edie, who used to chase him with a croquet mallet, and of Aunt

* Incidentally, Airy calculated the boundary between the U.S.A. and Canada.

Annie, who introduced to Woodbridge the letters W.C.T.U. and who to the end was staunch in her aversion to the first miracle, out of her own conviction that all wine should be turned to water.) Prejudice dies slowly in East Anglia, and the family was Roundhead to the core. The only palliative was that Cambridge had at some moments in times past struck great blows for non-conformity. Had it been Oxford! — but such a thought, at that time, was unthinkable.

(When I came down from Oxford my father remarked to me, as if it were a surprising meditation, " I've had three sons at Oxford, and it doesn't seem to have done them any particular harm.")

He went to Cambridge. It was Cambridge perhaps not at its best moment. (I speak subject to correction, and, as an Oxford man, I speak of course with diffidence.) It was a moment when King's was largely dominated by " the Eton push." Oscar Browning (" O.B.," as he was widely and affectionately known) to a considerable extent set the tone for the college. He fancied his chess, and at some party, with an intention that was kindly, he proposed a game as a way of drawing out the gauche and silent freshman. Fifty years later, when my father told me about it, he said: " I'm afraid I didn't understand. I was rather a lout. I made a fool of him."

Of course there were those college friendships which are godlike — those friendships which, when kept in repair, as Dr. Johnson puts it, remain the wine of life. There were Berry, Richmond, Chree, and Lowes Dickinson. I have no doubt whatever that there were high thoughts and a sufficiency of pleasant jest to add that wonderful savor to the plain living and the hard grind which only scholars of Cambridge (and possibly Oxford too) can wholly understand. In later years my father often revisited King's, and dined or stayed there, with affectionate pride. Yet from the preceding anecdote about O.B., and from the fact that he would rarely talk about his student days, I judge they were not wholly happy. Like Dr. Johnson, my father never cared to talk about the shifts and indignities to which a proud man may be put by poverty. Poor to the point of privation he certainly was. As far as I can make out, the main items of his diet were brown bread and marmalade, and not enough of that. The Dean of the College, in recommending him for a further Exhibition for his final year, wrote that "Frank Morley has been conspicuous for moderate habits and quiet industry." To be conspicuous by being inconspicuous is rarely, at the college stage, a mark of satisfaction. Nor, if I may judge from his later attitude toward examinations, did he take kindly to the Mathematical Tripos as it was then conducted. The evils of the Tripos have been sharply attacked (in that time by Clifford, and more lately by G. H. Hardy) and that dead hand, which did all it could to stifle Cambridge mathematics, has now been lifted. Then, the grip was strong. My father enjoyed competition — I should have mentioned that his one undergraduate distinction was that he was President of the Cambridge University Chess Club — but the nature of the Tripos competition was by no means congenial.

To make that clear, I must interrupt the narrative with a digression.

After my father's death it fell to me to go through his mathematical papers. For many years he had been head of the department of mathematics at The Johns Hopkins University in Baltimore, and later he had the freedom of a Professor Emeritus. I don't know how things are now in educational circles, but in the first third of this century, when teachers were much needed in the U.S.A., you were prevented from becoming a college teacher without a Doctor's degree, and a condition of obtaining that piece of parchment was the publication of a thesis which embodied a contribution to the sum of existing knowledge — a contribution which had to be described as new and original. It is debatable whether the ability to be a good teacher and the ability to perform new and original research are always correlated. In the academic way of things they were so correlated — not necessarily in perpetuity, but once in a lifetime, at least at the marvellous moment when the eggshell cracked and there emerged the fledgeling Doctor. Therefore the life of a head of a mathematics department at that period (things may have changed) was somewhat like the life of whatever bird it is (in legend, the pelican) which spends its day plucking feathers from its breast to cover its young. We had many family jests, and one of them was to call my father by the nickname " Doctors," partly because of the succession of shy guests who would appear in rotation for dinner at 2026 Park Avenue — " doctors " was what they had to be made into.

Once in a rare while there might be an exception. There might be one or more real mathematicians. There might even be a vintage year.

At The Johns Hopkins University, in the mathematical seminar, there was such a vintage year, the year 1902. Among the graduate students taking their degrees that year were no less than three who promised to be really creative. (One died too soon, one I have lost sight of, but the third has undeniably fulfilled that promise.) When I came to look through the examination papers my father had cared to preserve, I turned with some interest to see what sort of test he had set for the talented students of that year. Sure enough, it was one of the papers he had cared to keep. The little printed sheet dated 1902 was certainly a stiff examination. There were a couple of problems such as the ordinary fellow might have been expected to swot up, but that was merely to temper the wind. The main questions were on the very frontiers of mathematical thought; and what interested me more than the printed questions was the sentence which Doctors had added in his own handwriting at the top of each paper. The sentence was: " In this examination, if an exact answer does not suggest itself, an inspired guess will be of value."

In the midst of tedious and melancholy sifting of a dead man's papers (*Manetho, be thou with me!*), I laughed aloud. So typical was the instruction, so very much in keeping with Doctors' type of creativity. The quality of his mathematical writings for which I try to find an exact phrase, is something like *power informed by elegance*. In physical habits Doctors was not what might be called a tidy man. His study was always in confusion, even unto himself. He did not by any means know where everything was. He knew only the important things. On more than one occasion a dividend warrant, before getting so far as the bank, proved to be an irresistibly convenient book-marker.* Before we gave away his library we shook it very carefully, and solved questions which for thirty years had bothered accountants in three continents.† With his clothes, Doctors had a way of hitching them on which was perfectly designed to express a gentle criticism of conformity. Before going out to pay a call (those were days in which one paid calls and returned them) my mother would rightly insist on looking him over. I don't say that Madame Doctors (our natural nickname for her) ever actually made the hissing sound that hostlers make when they have in hand the curry-comb, but there was a sort of astral hiss about the operation. She would tighten his dark-green four-in-hand tie and straighten his coat-collar, while he would snort with indignation, and pull the ends of his big moustache, and look very fierce. Of course it did no good to pull his tie tight or straighten his collar. Before the call was over, in some marvellous way the tie would be far removed from the stud, the collar again awry.

At the dinner table Doctors had an unconscious habit of pushing away the knives and spoons and

* Footnote by Felix: why don't you say dividend checks? Answer by F.V.M.: because those which gave *me* most trouble were dividend warrants.

† The works of Salmon, Riemann, Clifford and Klein were especially rich pay-dirt.

forks so that in a short space of time his neatly laid
" place " looked like a battleground, and as he rarely
noticed which spoon or fork to use, he sometimes
ended with a somewhat puzzling relict. Everyone
else might notice the signals by which Madame Doctors might attempt to anticipate this evil, but never
he. Soup he was fond of, but (I say it with horror)
he was apt to make something of a succulent noise and
(worse and worse) a fringe of soup-drops was apt to
cling to that great moustache until at an exclamation
long suppressed but finally emergent from Madame
Doctors (the longer those exclamations were retained
the more energetically they would pop out) he would
sit up very straight, and quite deliberately disarrange
a little more the table silver, and then take his napkin
and ostentatiously, as if to some vast distant audience,
wipe off the offending drops, and look very fierce.

Yet if there was this unconcern as to outward habits (I hope I haven't made them sound repulsive, for
they weren't) there was, in the interior courtyard of
his mind, a natural elegance and an extraordinary
delicacy. There was an instantaneous perception, a
veritable sophistication of sensibility. You get a
glimpse of the quickness in the way he astonished the
friend who met him when he first arrived in America.
The ship docked at Philadelphia, and shortly after-
ward the two men were walking up Market Street.
There was a street-vendor with apples on a barrow,
with a large placard, " 3 for 5." My father instantly
stopped to ask the apple-seller, " Excuse me, which
do you mean? Three apples for five cents, or three
cents for five apples? " The apple-man made no

recorded answer, except to raise up the end of his barrow and hastily push off into a side-street. And you get a little of the delicate sophistication of my father's mind in the note he wrote his old friend Chree from Colorado Springs on his first visit to the Rocky Mountains. "I do not climb any mountains if I can help it," he wrote, "but I walk between them when they are well arranged with some enthusiasm." * These are oblique expressions of qualities which, conjoined with imaginative power, are observable throughout his mathematical writings.

So, to come back to my father's student days, I think I know what he most resented about the Mathematical Tripos at Cambridge. It was the mass of unco-ordinated stuff, unvitalized and unshaped, "which had to be done their way." "They used to fling it at you," he said, in one of our few conversations about the Cambridge education. I had the impression that the Tripos of his time meant incessant problems but few ideas; and the problems, I repeat, to be done *their* way. Behind him there was plenty of pressure (perhaps too much) to make a distinguished showing. He made the mistake of overworking and had a breakdown of some sort, serious enough to cause him to withdraw from college for a year. (When we were children and making too much racket my mother would occasionally allude to "brain

* My father had what is known as "a bad head for heights." At the mere thought of a potential precipice he would recoil. Felix says: "You might like to add a line about Doctors' courage in coming by bus from the Riviera to Geneva, around 'corniches,' which must have been horrible for him. That memorable summer at Geneva he was wont to refer frequently, and jocularly, to 'those corniches.'"

fever " with a hushed and alarming intonation.) His resultant place, the following year, among the Wranglers (which to a child was also an alarming word) was lower down than had been generally expected. To complete his woe he was not awarded a Fellowship.

At this long distance I cannot really feel too sorry about it, nor did my father in his later years. At the time it must have been a crashing blow.

Leave out the family sacrifices, the Woodbridge pride, the Airy pride. (Old long-lived Airy, still alive!) Consider only that whilst he was fully conscious of immortal longings he was debarred, through the absence of a Fellowship, from staying on at Cambridge — the Cambridge where his friends were staying — the Cambridge which, with whatever faults, was nevertheless the be-all and the end-all of English mathematicians. What else was there? Conscious of powers — yet in a right-little, tight-little world he had to seek a job upon the fringes.

In point of fact, the job was at Bath College. There proved to be compensations. But at the time my father took the job at Bath the compensations had not been revealed. All that he knew was that it was a job of cramming examination-stuff into schoolboys, and there would be no allowance for original research — no time to indulge inspired guesses.

Let me then pass to a prettier picture.

Chess.

4

Let us now praise famous men. . . .

Ecclesiasticus

MY FATHER went off chess for the year that he was out of college, but during the three years at Bath and until he left England in 1887, he seems to have played a good deal, and whenever he passed through London, despite the scarcity of half-crowns, he managed to place his stake upon the board and mix with the professionals at Simpson's Chess Divan. Famous Simpson's Divan! How I should have loved to see that old place in the Strand at the height of its dingy prime! Hallowed by memory of the immortal Morphy, that Lochinvar out of the West, who, like Mozart outdid his celebrated elders and won their hearts in the process! All except the heart of poor old Staunton, who could neither evade nor wholly avoid the threat that Morphy represented to his position of authority and all his vested interests! Simpson's I've known well in later mogrification, when the name connoted rare roast beef or a most delectable saddle of mutton, with Jim Bone across the table raising his tankard with a slight sidewise motion and a strong sidewise remark: " Frank, it has just come over me, you and I are the men my father warned me against. . . ." But, as the children say in a choosing game, even if you chose Jim Bone, the Simpson's of my generation was not the same as the Simpson's of the earlier age. After the purchase of the ancient Simpson's by the Savoy Hotel nothing further was known there about chessmen except the degenerate use of the Knight as a decorative motif in the lobby.* No, no matter how rare the beef or how well done the mutton, my Simpson's was not the same as the antediluvian smoke-filled room with its moth-eaten red plush settees (is this my imagination only?) and its stained marble-topped tables, at one of which, upon a battered board with battered chessmen my father would be playing with Old Bird.

Old Bird!— not much remembered now, I fancy, but well enough respected in those days, and apart from other things the originator of Bird's Bastard, an opening still very pleasing in its old-fashioned ding-dong way. Bird had written books. When he was in a difficulty he used to say: " It's all in my book — I'm sure the answer to that is in my book." He did get into difficulties, for he was a slashing fighter. He went for the throat. Frequently he got there. Sometimes he missed, but don't think he didn't know what he was doing. Don't think he didn't know his stuff. Always he was in there fighting with Blackburne and Horwitz, Lowenthal and Wisker, Zukertort and Steinitz, the tigers of those days.

* Doctors, if he had ever gone to the later Simpson's (which, being conspicuous for moderate habits, he never did) would certainly, at the sight of the Knight-décor, have looked very fierce, and quite possibly have said: " They *would* choose a Knight; a Rook would also have been suggestive."

At the time I write of, Steinitz was World's Champion at chess. Bird had the best score on record against him. In their adjourned match of 1867 this score can be read: STEINITZ, 8; BIRD, 7; Drawn, 7. Bird was not merely dashing. He could be patient and durable. Playing the Black men against Potter he won in 145 moves, in the then longest game on record. It occupied sixteen hours at four successive meetings, at Monfleet's, Newgate Street. That game was published in the *Field,* with Steinitz's notes, on May 31, 1879, " a rare study," as Bird himself remarks, " and a rich treat." But though he could be dogged, there was no *sitzfleisch* * in Bird's anatomy. It is clear that what his spirit most enjoyed was to " have at you." He was a sporting character, Old Bird, an old warhorse who said Ha ha among the trumpets, who smelled the battle far off, the thunder of the captains, and the shouting.

Would you care to see that verified, to see the sort of game they played at Simpson's in those days? On September 17, 1886, my father (presumably on the way back to Bath College after a vacation at Woodbridge) stopped off at Simpson's to play three games with Mr. Bird — for I ought to say that my father always referred to him, with fitting respect for the old professional, as " *Mr.* Bird." I don't know the order of the games. Here is the score of one of them. My father's annotations consist of two question

* *Sitzfleisch:* a term used in chess to indicate winning by use of the glutei muscles — the habit of remaining stolid in one's seat hour by hour, making moves that are sound but uninspired, until one's opponent blunders through boredom.

marks, at Mr. Bird's 5th and 12th moves. The remarks which I have ventured to insert are my own.

	White: F. M.	*Black:* Mr. Bird
1.	P — K 4	P — K 4
2.	Kt — K B 3	Kt — Q B 3
3.	P — Q 4	P × P
4.	Kt × P	B — B 4
5.	B — K 3	Q — R 5 (?)

That is the first of my father's question marks. For Black to move the Queen to the King's Rook's 5th, is usually, as in this case, a mistake. Yet it may be noted as an archaeological fact that when Blackburne adopted this same Scotch gambit three times in succession against Steinitz, Steinitz each time defended with Queen to King's Rook's 5th at his fourth move, and each time won. Bird was well aware of the riskiness, but he probably thought he could get away with it. He was a little scornful of the Scotch gambit. "There is not much in it," he remarks in his book on *Chess Practice* (published 1882); again, "the attack properly met is not very formidable." Perhaps; but why go in for the coming exchanges? I'm afraid Old Bird is playing badly.

6.	Kt — Q B 3	B × Kt
7.	B × B	Kt × B
8.	Q × Kt	Kt — B 3

This move of Black's is all very well, but where is the Black Queen to go if White presses, as he proceeds to do?

9.	K Kt P — Kt 3	Q — Kt 5

This gets the Black Queen on the diagonal Q B 1 to K R 6 — if she could stay there. But White can attack and develop at the same time and Black is going to pay for his cramped position.

Position after Black's 9th move

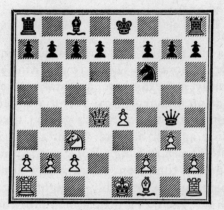

FIGURE 3

10.	B — K 2	Q — K 3
11.	P — K 5	Kt — Kt 1
12.	Castles (Q's side)	P — Q R 3 (?)

My father's second question mark. The move is almost unfair to Bird's memory. He must have foreseen White's 13th move. It is not a good game.

13.	B — Kt 4	Q — Q B 3
14.	P — K 6	Kt — B 3
15.	P × Q P ch.	B × P
16.	B × B ch.	Kt × B
17.	K R — K 1 ch.	K — Q 1
18.	Q × Kt P	....

Black is hog-tied and helpless.   All his moves are now forced.

18.	. . . .	R — K 1
19.	R × R ch.	K × R
20.	R — K 1 ch.	K — Q 1
21.	Q — Kt 8 ch.	

and White wins.

From that particular game you would think the roles of the players were reversed.   The young amateur takes hold of an opportunity and gives the old professional a very accurate and scientific trouncing. But don't waste your sorrow on Old Bird.   My father goes on to mention that " Mr. Bird won two games."   Though Mr. Bird was kind enough to mention to other people that my father was a hard man to beat.   I think that is evident from the above game. White's play is energetic in the grand old manner. Black's carelessness (even old professionals have lapses) is instantly and ruthlessly exploited, until he is wiped up as a man wipeth a dish, wiping it and turning it upside down.

(Which description by Isaiah * is incidentally a very good description of the way in which my father, on Sunday nights in later years, wiped dishes.)

* Footnote by Gerald W. Johnson: Not Isaiah; Second Kings 21:13.

5

Forty years on, when afar and asunder . . .
Edward E. Bowen, *Harrow Football Song*

WHEN my father moved to North America, when he
became Professor of Mathematics at Haverford
College, when he brought his English bride (whom
he had met at Bath) to the mild, friendly, musical *
atmosphere of Haverford in its most golden decade,
when any rugosities of upbringing and any chips upon

* Footnote by Felix: " You must change the word ' musical.' I
suggest ' tranquil ' as a substitute. Whatever the advantages of Haverford in 1890, a musical atmosphere was not among them. In fact,
one of the greatest services Mother and Dad did for the College was
to introduce that atmosphere, as many of the old-timers recall. This
is referred to in Rufus Jones' history of Haverford. Recall that
shortly before this David Bispham was not allowed to play the violin †
on the campus, and that Doctors really organized the Haverford
College Glee Club, supplemented by the musical evenings which they
initiated at ' Westward Ho.' "

† Footnote by Christopher: " Not violin; zither. § He used to
leave the College campus and go to the Haverford railroad station in
order to play it."

§ Footnote by F.V.M.: I welcome Felix's comment (with Christopher's insertion) but I have not altered the word " musical " for
the following reason. Haverford, as well as being the site of Haverford College, was a residential neighbourhood. I will admit to an
ambiguity. Felix thinks primarily of the College, but I was thinking of the young English couple set down in a new world. The
College wasn't musical until they made it so, but the neighbourhood
was musical, and most of the friends they quickly found, were dis-
tinctly so. I need mention only one family to prove my point:
the Charlton Yarnalls.

[28]

the shoulder just quietly reduced themselves to humorous dimensions, when in the midst of his first large endeavour in the realm of Analytic Functions he also had time for geometric fancies, and the fancies came — when in all ways life was so happily expanding for him — he gave up chess.

That is the sort of paragraph which gives great satisfaction to an impetuous writer who is anxious to get on with his argument. See the ground it covers! — it skips from England to America, takes in about ten years of time, and brings us almost to the moment when I can begin to take a personal interest in the story. Yet, in criticism, what a left-handed way in which to introduce one's own mother; and what a concealment of the great truth I mentioned some time ago, that you never know what may happen when you begin to play chess.

My mother's maiden name was Bird. Her father, James Bird Esq., had a modest country seat at Hayward's Heath in Sussex. Gone were the earlier spacious days when the two families of Bird and Clay, inhabiting adjacent large estates at Muswell Hill and Crouch End, made a very prosperous amalgamation; gone were the days of the large Town houses in Great Cumberland Place, and 49 Montague Place, where my mother was born. James Bird was a delightful dilettante, not altogether helped, perhaps, by his attendance on Court life as a young man, yet not spoiled by that either, except that it became a matter of increasing agitation that an inscrutable fate prevented him from maintaining his large family in the style to which he himself had been accustomed. The steady

Clays hung on to their patrimony; the volatile Birds did not seem to do so. Not that Hayward's Heath was to be sneered at. By comparison with previous glories it was a modest corner, but anyone could see it was a Gentleman's Seat. And to do the old Gentleman credit, he did his best to see that each of his children had the best individual teaching to develop their talents.

My mother's aptitude was for the violin. While she was still at Miss Smith's Academy, Nilghari Villa, Brighton, she was also playing first violin, a tall shy schoolgirl in white dress and long black stockings, with the Brighton orchestra. And the teacher who bustled her into that was nobody less than M. Jacoby. It was during the period in which Jacoby was conducting the Alhambra orchestra, and writing a hundred ballets and divertissements, and many comedy-operas (including *The Black Crook*), that he found time to teach many students, including my mother. Turning out some old sheet-music in a recent move, I came across a manuscript, written out most carefully and neatly in the Master's hand. The title-page reads as follows:

DUETT for

VIOLIN and PIANO

dedicated to his talented

pupil

Miss Lilly Bird

by

M. Jacoby

Decbr. 1875

My mother, at that date, was nine years old. A decade after that, when my mother went to stay with the Sherwoods in Bath, her well-practised violin was under her arm. She may have given some lessons; I know she played to the boys of Bath College. I would wager that when the instructor of mathematics came up to her, the question of her relationship to Old Bird formed an easy conversational gambit, and paved the way towards the union of two shy, sensitive, and strangely loving spirits.

Such are the omissions if you try to go too fast. My mother often complained that her schooling had been inadequate, that at Miss Smith's Academy all that was taught was the scandalous lives of the Kings of England; and I would think that M. Jacoby was fully as important in drawing her out as, in my father's school-days, G. B. Airy was to him. How wonderfully active, as one looks back upon them, were those Victorian professionals! What a bustling period! No matter how shy and retiring my mother might be (as a girl she was morbidly self-conscious) Jacoby would have none of it, no nonsense, poohpoohed it all, popped her into the orchestra — and there she was, playing away for dear life in support of no less a soloist than Madame Norman Neruda.* The noble self-reliance which she learned that way was somewhat lost in later years, when the domestic struggle with three children, the fear of disturbing

* My mother's nature rivalled my father's, in the possession of sensitive, curious quirks. Her full maiden name was Lilian Janet Bird, the Lilian spelt with one L in the middle. I am pretty sure the reason why none of her sons ever, in her lifetime, saw M. Jacoby's " Duett," was that he spelt her name " Miss Lilly."

Doctors at his work, and finally the onset of a painful type of neuritis, caused her to lay aside the fiddle. But the joy of the musical evenings in the long Haverford honeymoon is something I still hear spoken of by old Philadelphia friends.

That halcyon period on the Haverford campus is something I never knew.* My brothers, absorbent as children are, had an inkling of it. Scrutinize the mature actions of Christopher and Felix, and you will notice an observable persistence of desire for identification with Haverford. There wouldn't be such a strong desire, or so persistent, unless Haverford had been beautiful to them as children, and it couldn't have meant so much to them as children if it had not had an even fuller meaning to the parents. To my father and mother what it meant, in a single word, was fruition. It was a Forest of Arden existence which comprised elemental things: mathematics, music, children, friends.

So my father gave up chess. He didn't need it.

He gave up serious chess. Of course he played with Uncle Spiers, with Walter Shipley and other Quaker worthies, and of course when Emanuel Lasker, then succeeding Steinitz as World's Champion, came to stay overnight at Haverford, my father (who knew him as a mathematician) played with him. As a matter of fact, my father won the game they played, but he always attributed that to some courteous idea of Lasker's of repaying hospitality. Which may have been so, for Lasker had too much

* "It is an extremely rare thing to see a halcyon." Aristotle, *History of Animals,* 5, 9.

chess-genius to have been caught napping by the deceptive innocence of the Friendly atmosphere. I don't wish to overstate the episode. From all of the foregoing I merely want to establish that my father was a hard-hitting chess player who in his time had studied the game seriously, but who in his mature life, and for understandable reasons, had given it up. I have also tried to establish that the pursuit of the game for the sake of the game had some observable social impacts on the course of his life.

It was Polybius who taught me how valuable it is, in writing history, to pause and state just where you are in the analysis, and what you are trying to do. I am about half way toward establishing what chess is, and two-fifths of the way toward the reason for suggesting a change.

By the turn of the century the Haverford period was over. We moved to Baltimore. My father's position at The Johns Hopkins University was more important than it had been at Haverford, and in many ways it was more of a chore. I have spoken of the procession of students; some pleasant friendships developed from that procession. There was also a procession of manuscripts which came to him in his capacity as editor of the American Journal of Mathematics; the foreign stamps were a great stimulus to our stamp-collections. But raising money for the Department of Mathematics was a less agreeable activity. In my father's lectures he had a flair for the dramatic, but it was entirely the drama of the argument itself, the mathematical keys at a given moment tumbling into an unexpected combination; apart from that he was no showman and no salesman. Professors who made use of physical equipment had an easier task in extracting money from the citizens of Baltimore. Certainly nobody ever needed less physical equipment than my father. If you watched him, as a contemplative child might watch a large, strange, friendly animal which had emerged from its den, you would see that whatever book he might be reading would presently be laid down, and except that his blue eyes were open, and that once in a while he would pull at his nose with his thumb and forefinger, he might be just about to go to sleep; and then he would begin to fiddle in his waistcoat pocket for a stub of pencil perhaps two inches long, and there would be a certain amount of scrabbling in a side pocket for an old envelope, and then there would be silence for a long time; until he would get up a little stealthily and make his way toward his study — but the boards in the hall always creaked, and my mother would call out, " Frank, you're not going to work ! " — and the answer would always be, " A little, not much ! " — and the study door would close.

(It wasn't hard to gather that my father was working at geometry, and I knew pretty well what geometry was, because for a long time I had been drawing triangles and things; but when you examined the envelope he left behind, what was really mysterious was that there was hardly ever a drawing on it, but just a lot of calculations in Greek letters. Geometry without pictures I found it hard to approve; indeed, I prefer it with pictures to this present day.)

Doctors — we have now come round again to the

time when the nickname is appropriate — was forty years older than I, and when I was old enough to know him not merely as a parent but as a friend; he was a humorous, mellow, graying man with an impressively high forehead and a big drooping moustache (now white) and the same unconscious habit of disarranging his place at table, and the same old trick of standing very straight and attempting to look very fierce if anybody interfered with his neck-tie or his coat-collar. In spite of his pretended fierceness I knew that he was exquisitely gentle. His literary taste was mild to the point of prudery; in every art he instinctively recoiled from anything ambitious, harsh, or startling; he thought it was effrontery when G. H. Hardy called a book, without further qualification, *Pure Mathematics;* and he was positively shocked when Walter de la Mare, who happened to be staying with us, mentioned in conversation with Mrs. Turnbull, then an old lady, the word " death." *

One of the most astonishing blasphemies I ever heard was innocently cooked up by Doctors, and later on gravely repeated to me by Madame Doctors, to the effect that Christ couldn't be held to speak with real authority, because He wasn't married and didn't

* Footnote by Christopher: " re the prudishness of literary tastes: I've never forgotten that when a Freshman at Haverford I discovered *Tom Jones* in the college library (I had to get special permission to read it, because it was supposed to be saved until one was Sophomore!) and was so enchanted and amused by it that I burst out in enthusiasm to Doctors about it. He remarked, very positively, ' I don't associate with stable-boys in life, and I don't intend to in literature.' . . . But listen: Doctors didn't just *pretend* to look fierce. He terribly *did!* "

have three children. The theory that an educator should be married was one of Doctors' firmest crotchets. He had many. We never had a decent dictionary, because he considered that a dictionary was the tool of a lazy man. If you had a proper grounding in Greek and Latin you could discern for yourself the roots, and the spelling, of most words. He had that grounding, and never forgot what he had learned, and I recall being very proud of the way he would read over with me, and make clear, some passage that I found difficult in Xenophon or Virgil. But he was a little like my son Oliver, who, when a child, would never read a book that he hadn't read before. If in discovering the classics I got off his beat, he wouldn't be much interested. In principle, though, he respected the classics. " Works that have stood the test of time are probably worth reading," he would say. " Customs change, but people haven't changed much. Americans, though, are something new in a way. They are very alert, and they won't learn from the past. They are like clever children — clever children." As an aid to reflection he would pull at his nose, and Madame Doctors, who disapproved that habit, would say, " Don't do that, Frank."

As I look back, it seems to me that Doctors' view of the outside world was just about as limited as that of most men who concentrate on their own ordinary business; that is to say, he had convictions which were strong in inverse proportion to his experience or knowledge. I had a great passion to explore as many kinds of life as possible, and when I would return from a summer of dory-fishing off Nantucket, or from the Franklin Motor Car factory at Syracuse, or from working as a steward on the Canadian-Pacific route from Vancouver to Alaska, and express to him an indignation at some of the observable brutalities of our capitalist society, he would suggest that when I had seen more of life I would learn to accept it more placidly. " Capitalism hasn't done too badly by me," he would say, " and by the way, I hope you learn to cotton on to the idea of compound interest." When he had only small stakes to play with, he himself had cottoned on to that idea all right. Aside from the habit I've mentioned about book-markers, his head for ordinary business was well screwed on. " Think of being busted," I can almost hear him saying. " Think of being busted, higher than a kite." * He was no salesman, but he was a shrewd buyer.

* I have noted that Doctors had a bad head for heights, and in the family that was so axiomatic that it lent a humorous overlay to the phrase in the text. At the simple three-handed card-games, which I used to play with him and Madame Doctors, whenever he was in difficulties it was a favourite expression. " Busted," he would say; and with increasing poignancy, " busted — higher than a kite! " At which, if Madame Doctors was winning — as frequently was the case, for at simple card-games she was very cunning — her lips would twitch for a smile; and I would say, " Now, Mother, don't laugh about it! " And she would say, with indignation, " I'm *not* laughing! " To which there was the quite absurd traditional rejoinder: " You *are*, Madame Doctors, I can see you are, you are *laughing like a hyena!* " Which for some reason which is wrop in mystery, and which was no doubt aided by the prospect, soon to be demonstrated, of her winning, would never fail to send Madame Doctors off into her most infectious laughter. I should have thought such homespun gaiety was incommunicable to children, if it had not been for a remark of my son Donald, who at the age of six, when he was told of the birth of a sister, said: " Give her a young, gay name — like Lily! " There's tribute to a grandmother!

Doctors always lived below his means, and yet, within an over-all strict discipline, he allowed himself an occasional romantic flutter. To my brother Felix, as a most careful Executor and a Bank Director in his own right, these occasional vagaries of investment with most alluring names (The Wayne Natatorium, The Arroyo Rico Gold Mining and Milling Company, The Gaspereau Silver Fox Farm, The Big Horn Collieries) must have been an exasperation, even to the point of showing up Doctors' judgement in a horrid lurid light. But in the general range of his investments these excursions were rare, and I am sure they represented a realm of deliberate and conscious self-indulgence, an identification with geography (he loved such names as Sonora, Mexico; the Minas Basin; Colorado) and a happy adventurous contact with an outside world which retained a colour from boyhood memories of W. Stephens Hayward, Mayne Reid and "Gascoyne, the Sandalwood Trader." The character which he invented as his contribution to the family newspaper (which was perpetually, though sporadically, appearing under the banner: THE FAMILY NEWS, Editor: Christopher D. Morley; Assistant Editor: Felix M. Morley; Assistant Assistant Editor: Frank V. Morley) was an ingenious and adventurous explorer called Captain Rosebud. It was Doctors in the character of Captain Rosebud who would gallantly stake his claim on the Arroyo Rico, and vicariously refresh exhausted muscles in the Wayne Natatorium.

For the most part Doctors retired from the outside world — but indeed, that phrase is not strong enough

— he was retracted from within to dwell with mathematical abstractions. I suppose that many people who don't know much about mathematics or abstractions may think that was a perfect refuge, an understandable " flight from reality," for a man of his sensitivity and delicacy. Call it that if you like, but it was nothing of the kind; it was something positive, not negative. I don't think Doctors knew a great deal about the outer world, though he coped with it shrewdly. I do think he knew a good deal about the interior world, not from outward pressure, but from its own inward pulsation. It was always true of Doctors that the graces of mathematics, the pleasant questions and elegant and unexpected answers, never failed to interest him. His gift for, so to speak, the lyric, the song, the short piece, is demonstrable. That places him in the Lyra Mathematica and goes well enough with the outward picture as I have drawn it. But more than that picture might indicate, he was actually in thrall from within. Power in mathematics is not your power; you are in its power. You don't turn it on or off at your will; it turns on you. It is not an 'escape from reality; the power is the reality; everything else is less real. Power, whether pure or impure, is difficult to cope with, whether for the coper or the coped. Having spoken so much about Doctors' gentleness I must in fairness also mention this power, which in itself, undisciplined, ungeared, can be a roaring, raging, wasting sickness. I don't want to be fanciful, and am still attempting to be accurate, when I say that a transcendent description of the initial nagging, the subsequent endurance, and the final resolution of a mathematical urge is provided (if, which isn't necessary, you should wish to interpret it that way) in that late Beethoven Sonata in C Minor, Op. III. For my money, that is a very exact sensuous transcription of a swift, teasing, and successful course of the disease. When the nagging is unsuccessful, unresolved, the matter is far otherwise. When the power is ungeared and the mind feels without seeing and sees without feeling, then it is no pleasant retreat to the possessor, and no gift, but just a cold boiling of hen scraps.

It was Doctors' good fortune that spontaneous creation rarely failed him. So far as I know, he had few blank periods. It was my good fortune that as I grew up I was able to ask some pertinent questions, and start up a number of hares. In mathematics we had tremendous fun working together, or, when separated, still working by means of voluminous correspondence, at that most innocent of blood-sports. There was I with my pea-shooter, starting up something I might be unable to identify; and there was Captain Rosebud with a full professional armoury, trailing the thing from this side and that, and quite often what had seemed to be a hare at the beginning would turn out to be a rhinoceros by the time it was bagged. For twenty years, on and off, we worked together, and wrote a book together, and shaped many things with mutual pleasure. And now, after all that long explanation, I am ready to come back to chess.

During the twenty years that Doctors and I worked together, as one of several games that we played for relaxation, sometimes we tried chess.

The chess was always at my suggestion. It was never satisfactory. I was never able to give him a good enough game.

While I would be collecting the faded old chess-board which had fallen into two halves and the red and white striped cloth bag with a draw-string in which the fine old chessmen always lived, Doctors would reach for a book (probably *Middlemarch*). I would set up the men and attract his attention. "Ah!" he would say, "is this serious?" I might indicate that this time it was indeed going to be a serious test of his powers. "Too bad," he would say; "you can't expect me at my time of life to be serious." So he would make a move and return to his book. Some time later, if I could get any purchase at all on the game, Doctors might lay down the book very gently, and put his pipe beside it as gingerly as if it were made of thistledown. "Ah! that's a pity," he would say; and after a pause, "I was afraid of that. I'll offer you a draw." When I refused the draw, as I always did (I was young) he would move, and go on reading. And at the sad inevitable end, when the book was lowered for the last time, Doctors would put his head a little on one side and with thumb and forefinger pull at his nose, and Madame Doctors would look up from her knitting and say, "Don't do that, Frank," and as the poor cut snake (that's me) was slowly writhing on the pitchfork he would continue to pull at his nose and remark: "I studied it too much for you to beat me. But I advise you not to study chess. It can get too absorbing."

So that was how it was. At chess, there was too much power for me to cope with. Unlike Mr. Bird, never could I come back from a crushing defeat and win two games. But you mustn't get me wrong, any more than my father. I wasn't an absolute duffer, nor wholly a sheep in sheep's clothing. My trouble wasn't altogether that of Morris Finsbury in *The Wrong Box:* " I fear it seems too ramified for a person of my powers of mind." In the wider ramifications of mathematics Doctors and I did find mutual creativity.

Why were we not able to find in chess the mutual enjoyment which we could and did find in other forms of work and play?

6

All things come from that one source, from that ruling Reason of the Universe, either under a primary impulse from it or by way of consequence. . . .

Marcus Aurelius, VI, 36.

I AM increasingly convinced that this is a very peculiar treatise on chess, and if we are to go right to the root of the matter I shall have to continue to handle my thoughts, as I have done so far, with exemplary firmness.

I think I have established that when you start to play chess you never know what's going to happen, and whatever social implications may occur are in a sense part of the game. But the exact nature of the game itself hasn't yet been established. We have started a hare — or what we think is a hare — but we haven't yet bagged it. I think we should track it from a different direction. That was where Doctors had it all over me in mathematics. My notion was to run the short way; that the short way was the way of Nature. His, by comparison, and in the words of Marcus Aurelius, was to "look at the yawning gulf of Time behind thee, and before thee at another Infinity to come." He used to go to what seemed to me the darndest distances. If I now proceed to go too far, it's a trick that should be blamed on him.

I want to go so far as Manetho. Manetho has been in my head all through this inquiry. And as Doctors used to say, " it must be relevant, else why should I go on thinking about it? "

I'll admit that Manetho, unless you happen to have been thinking of him lately, seems a far cry. Manetho was an Egyptian priest who flourished in the third century, B.C. (Flourished — it is a gay word — I heartily enjoy the pleasantries of scholars — I have known those who would write: " The *floruit* of Manetho fell in the reign of Philadelphus. . . .") But there are certain facts about the twenty-three hundred year old Manetho which appeal to me intimately. One is that while he was extremely fond of Herodotus, he found occasion to criticise him as an historian, even while recognizing his literary eminence and applauding his general gusto. Herodotus has sometimes reminded me of Christopher. Another is, Manetho was not above arguing cats and dogs with Philadelphus — which is as reasonable an identification as you might find for brother Felix. A third is that Manetho was custodian of the hieroglyphic records which none but an Egyptian priest could read, and that was why his name kept coming to me in that sad time when, among the family, it fell to me to pack away all of Doctors' mathematical papers which I thought worth preserving, and which are still packed away, awaiting I don't know what.

Herodotus, who hounded Manetho into publication, said of the Egyptians who lived in the cultivated country, that they were " the most diligent of all men in preserving the memory of the past, and far better skilled in chronicles than any others whom I have questioned." * Well, a difference shows up there, for I have not been very diligent about the past and, as in this essay, am much more interested in the future. But I do find a special pleasure in Manetho which makes me partial to him. He observed that the ancient land of Egypt was being invaded by a lot of clever Greeks, who were alert and energetic, intelligent and ignorant, and instead of sitting in his club-window he said to himself, how can you expect them to know what Egypt was and is and will be, unless we tell them? To tell, is never easy. Suppose you're conscious of a debt to pay, and manfully you try to pay it, how can you do so if there is no common coin to pay it in, no common references, no common language? Manetho was a would-be torchbearer, but nobody bothered very much to pick up his torch. Scarcely a shred or particle remains of his own writings, and the reasons for the survival of his name are first, the almost accidental importance of his chronology to the Jewish historians (notably Josephus, but we needn't go into that here), and second, the difficulty which he presents to scholars. On the second score he is delectably remembered for various cries of agony and anguish; such as the cry of Boeckh, which, in the face of the complicated pressures which beset the ordinary fellow of today, I find delicious — " Never," cries Boeckh, " has there arisen a more complicated problem than that of Manetho." (*Manetho und die Hundssternperiode,* 1845, p. 10.) Doesn't that want to make you find out about Manetho? Even if

* Herodotus, ii. 77, 1.

you are not influenced by the lovely lament of Hermes
Trismegistus, as to the inevitable failure of communication of the values of one civilisation to another: " O Aegypte, Aegypte, religionum tuarum
solae supererunt fabulae, eaeque incredibiles posteris
tuis; solaque supererunt verba lapidibus incisa, tua
pia facta narrantibus." [" O Egypt, Egypt, of thy
religious rites nought will survive but idle tales which
thy children's children will not believe; nought will
survive but words graven upon stones that tell of thy
piety."] *

Although scarcely a shred remains of the original
text of Manetho — only so much as is left of a man
who is torn by crocodiles — he still possesses, against
the mocking laughter of the Fates, the poetry which
sometimes flowers in a lonely phrase. I don't mean
a mere archaic quaintness, though I find that pleasant
enough, for instance in the title of one of his scraps,
On the Making of Kyphi. I mean the real startling
stuff of poetry, as in the phrase " he built the many-
chambered Labyrinth as his tomb." How rightly
does Professor Waddell fall upon Karst for translat-
ing the word here given as " many-chambered " by
the expression " das höhlenwendelgangförmige. . . ."
" He built the many-chambered Labyrinth as his
tomb " could come right out of Dante. And yet, all

* The Latin Asclepius III. 25, in W. Scott, *Hermetica,* i. 1924,
p. 342. Lest anybody be taken in by my pretended scholarship, I
wish to point out that most of the references in this section are
pinched from one of my favourite volumes in the Loeb Classical
Library: *Manetho,* with an English translation by W. G. Waddell,
Professor of Classics in Fuad el Awal University, Cairo, Egypt, Har-
vard University Press and William Heinemann Ltd., MCMXL.

that's in passing. It isn't for anything that I've said so far that I need Manetho in this chess manual. Of course I need such an interest as he displayed in the attempt to communicate to posterity (although posterity didn't behave in the way Manetho wanted it to). But the reference which I here specifically need, the exact and precise reason for straying so far as Manetho, has not yet been mentioned.

Specifically and precisely, it is Manetho's devotion to the cult of Serapis.

Most happily and fortunately, we don't in the least need to bother to discuss what was the cult of Serapis.

It is enough to know that Manetho was devoted to it, and that the cult of Serapis was a dromenon.

". . . a dromenon, a pattern of dynamic expression in which the performers express something larger than themselves, beyond their powers of speech to express and a therapeutic rhythm in which they find release and fulfillment. . . ." So says Jane Harrison, in *Ancient Art and Ritual*.

That is what I have been searching for, for the understanding of the nature of chess. That is what I need at this point — the conception of a dromenon. I need the conception from a sufficient distance of time and space. I need it in the right size, with enough but not too much emotional content. It seems to me that Manetho hands me a torch I can pick up.

I hope so. With a parting wave to Manetho and to his forgotten cult of Serapis, I now return with fresh attention to the hare that we started. I return to chess as a dromenon.

7

The heavens call to you and around you glide
In circle, and their eternal beauties show,
And with earth only is your eye satisfied,
Wherefore he who discerns all battereth you.

Purgatorio, XIV 148–151 (translated by
Laurence Binyon)

THE position so far reached is this. I started with
the notion that chess when studied seriously is no
longer an innocent, friendly game. That seemed to
me a pity. The philosophy of having innocent fun
is not the same as the philosophy of having superior
technical equipment, and a first axiom of having fun is
that a little knowledge is a good thing and too much
knowledge isn't. On that, so far as chess goes, a
number of experts and duffers are agreed. It seemed
to me to illustrate the point to explain how my father
and I, who were much in sympathy, and who in other
realms created things together, at chess were separated not merely by his superior power, but by his
learning. I asked the question why, at chess, should
we be so separated. If anybody could have tempered
his knowledge to the occasion, Doctors would have
done so. But that is what you can't do. The second
and concealed axiom is that if you can play you must
play, and you must play as hard as you can. What

emerges from that axiom is that the game may demand from the players perhaps more than the players wish to demand from the game. What emerges is that chess is not merely a game but a dromenon.

That could have been stated without so much elaboration. It is obvious that both parties to a chess game play not merely against the human opponent, but also to make the best abstract use of the position of the pieces. Chess in its lesser part is a matter of traps, temptations, devices against the mortal frailty of your opponent. In greater part it is something demonstrated by both players against the setting of the universe, the chaste stars, the army of unalterable law. It is when the patterns of power, breaking and reforming as in a kaleidoscope, when pressures half revealed and half perceived manifest themselves and melt and shift, when there is imagination, elegance and accuracy not merely in the combinations but in the opposition and relationship of combinations — accuracy in the relationships which are invariant although the combinations differ — then and then only do the pieces come to life; then and then only do the players make together something which is both a battle and a ballet, and which in its unearthly beauty entirely transcends the little bits of carvings advancing and retreating on the parti-coloured board.

Chess is a dromenon. That's why it is inexorable. You can't play down to a weaker opponent.

You can't really play chess, that is, mutually create a good game, with anyone who is on a different level. A first-class player can't play chess with a second-class player; second-class can't play with third;

and third can't play with steerage. More precisely, steerage cannot create a good enough game with third-class, third-class with second, second with first. The players can beat or be beaten, but unless they are of the same class they cannot together create a game of chess which comes alive, which is a worthy ballet and battle in the sight of the chaste stars, the universe, and the unalterable law.

Chiamavi 'l cielo e 'ntorno vi si gira — the heavens call to you and around you glide in circle. The stars look down. And, as in any scene that needs two actors, one alone can't carry it. At chess, each has to play up to his opponent. Each player has to run like him who wins, and neither player run like him who loses. Each has to *be* the winner, until that ravishing moment, rarely noticeable to beginners but among master-players observed with an exquisite courtesy, when one of them resigns. And then the suffering is never wholly that one has been beaten by a stronger player. To be beaten by another man is nothing to be proud of; but it is more sad to fail the ruling Reason of the Universe, to fail the stars.

One of the corollaries to that is, that where there is learning or the will to learn, it can't be abolished without degeneration. "The Master said, Yu, have you ever been told of the Six Sayings about the Six Degenerations? Tzu-lu replied, No, never. The Master said, Come, then; I will tell you. Love of goodness without love of learning degenerates into silliness. Love of wisdom without love of learning degenerates into utter lack of principle. Love of keeping promises without love of learning degenerates into villainy. Love of uprightness without love of learning degenerates into harshness. Love of courage without love of learning degenerates into turbulence. Love of courage without love of learning degenerates into mere recklessness." * Which is even so at chess. Also applicable to this discussion is another quotation from the same Master: " To men who have risen at all above the middling sort, one may talk of things higher yet; but to men who are at all below the middling sort it is useless to talk of things that are above them."

It seems that we have to accept these harsh facts. It is the nature of the beast that we are dealing with. Unless something can be done about it, it all sounds very bad for my side, for the feeble folk, the conies, the spider and the grasshopper, the gallant amateurs.

* *Analects of Confucius*, Book XVII, translated by Arthur Waley. The two loves of courage is not a printer's error. The further quotation is from Book VI.

8

> I shall profre you large profres sayd syr Launcelot. I shall
> unarme my heed and the lyft quarter of my body, all that
> maye be unarmyd, and lete bynde my lyfte honde behynde
> me, so that it shall not helpe me, and ryghte so I shal do
> batayle wyth you. . . .
>
> *Morte d'Arthur*, The XIX Boke.

SOMETHING of course can be done at chess to iron
out the inequality between two players by handicapping the stronger.

A common scale of odds is for a stronger player
to offer a pawn and the first move, a pawn and two
moves, a knight, a rook, or two minor pieces. This
scale sets up no less than six classes of players, the
relative strength of each class being reckoned as of
the difference of a pawn and move. (The second
class would give pawn and move to the third class,
pawn and two moves to the fourth, knight to the
fifth, rook to the sixth; the other classes being ad-
justed in like proportion.) Handicap tournaments
have frequently been organized on this scale. Among
friends other ingenious handicaps have often been
arranged. Happy were those Christmas Feasts I remember at Trinity College (once again I have re-
verted to Cambridge) where according to their established custom Hardy would each year attempt to

harness Kapitza with some newly thought-up device; and a pleasure it was to watch Kapitza slowly and protestingly exert his strength toward escape and eventual mastery.

There should be no false shame about accepting odds, but there frequently is. If Doctors were alive I should now accept at least a knight from him if that would make a good game; but at the age of twenty I didn't want to accept anything. If I were now to meet Mr. Alekhin I'd accept any odds he might offer for the honor of playing with him at all; but I would want to know he was Mr. Alekhin. If it was just a stranger who said he was Mr. Alekhin that might be different. It is only when both players know and accept their respective places that they can know what odds to give or take. With those who reject the classification, the mere suggestion of odds is a slur direct. Two acquaintances A and B live in the same suburb, and chess is mentioned. Sure, says A, I watched you playing against Z, and I'll give you a rook. So you think you're that much better, says B; and a beautiful friendship is shattered.

More profoundly, the suggestion of odds is an impertinence toward the realm of the spirit. It is an acceptance of the despotism of experience, a denial of the possibility of inspiration, a resignation to the old dispensation. Who shall presume to determine in advance that state of life, unto which it shall please God to call me?

And the game of chess itself, the dromenon, rebels against the type of odds above-mentioned. There are some games, for example Go and Go-moku, where the arrangement of an initial handicap does not alter the game itself. (For that very reason, the philosophies reflected in Go and Go-moku seem sinister to me.) At chess, to remove a piece at the beginning is obviously to commit mayhem. Such an initial mutilation is unsymmetrical and displeasing. It could occur. Ugly and accidental malformations have to be faced. But nobody can say they are desirable. They are a distortion of the ideal.

Any method of handicapping by removing pieces doesn't suit with the philosophy of having fun, and doesn't suit with the nature of chess.

If chess develops such a rigid caste system as to separate parent from son, and if you can't correct it by any scheme of handicaps, why not just give it up?

Written in red chalk on the wall of a greengrocer's near Marylebone in London, all in one hand, I read this:

I love HENRY the rotten swine

A very singular and compact and startling declaration, don't you think?

I don't want to give it up.

9

Sleepe after toyle, port after stormie seas,
Ease after warre. . . .

The Faerie Queene, I, ix, 40

AT THE time when Doctors and I worked together at mathematics we were under no severe pressure. Perhaps that is partly why we never bothered to consider chess as a therapy, and therefore never examined the problem of the disparity of power.

We had another therapy or, if you prefer the word, another dromenon. We had the Book. The Book began when I was seventeen. It was to be a one-volume mathematical education, complete in itself. It was to be a high-road, driving from elementary geometry straight through the Theory of Functions. It was to be *my* education. It was to be (and was) my main contribution to modern mathematics. Modern mathematics had developed so rapidly that there was need for an up-to-date paideuma, a modern pedagogy. So that was to be my part — I was to be guinea-pig and amanuensis. It was a part most happily accepted. In the winter Doctors would work up his notes, and during the summer I would expand them into fair copy, and supply diagrams, and boggle over this and that, and get excited about some byway leading off the high-road.

The by-ways were a problem. I have to confess that we kept on straying off the high-road into some pleasant field, and picknicking there, when, as explorers with proper ambition, we ought to have been roaring northward all the while. We were not unaware of this, and would lecture each other and vow to reform, and for some stages plunge ahead with energy and discipline, but only to find ourselves again straying, and attempting to tuck into the vehicle, along with all the solid provisions, the various pretty wild-flowers we had gathered by the way. Each subsequent winter Doctors would go over and expand the fair copy I had made the previous summer; each subsequent summer I would go over and expand the hash that during the winter he had made of my previous manuscript. In its many transformations the quantity of manuscript grew and waxed right mightily. Some summers I would type it all afresh, putting in the symbols by hand. One summer I tried to use a Hammond typewriter, which was supposed to supply symbols of its own. But most summers I would copy out the new draft by hand from beginning to end. One way or another, each autumn there never failed to be a new and complete fair copy, which was duck soup for Doctors throughout the winter. Merrily would he alter, add to, and emend.

The affairs of the outside world caused surprisingly little interruption to this established routine. The First World War meant some delay, but in 1919 we resumed, and after 1920 the only difference made by my going to Oxford, and by my remaining in England, was that Doctors and Madame Doctors each summer crossed the Atlantic. Even by the early twenties the manuscript had reached such proportions as to constitute a formidable problem for Madame Doctors' packing. I don't think her peace of mind was improved by Doctors' reiterated instruction: " Remember, if the ship sinks the manuscript is to be saved. It's more important than we are." The only practical measure Madame Doctors could devise against so dread a possibility, was to have a large star painted on the steamer-trunk which contained the precious papers; and a succession of stewards was so earnestly impressed with the importance of saving the trunk with the star, that very likely there developed a tradition that the thing contained gold bullion — which might indeed have been a fair deduction from the weight of the trunk and from the manner in which it was so carefully kept locked.

When I would have notice that Doctors and Madame Doctors and the trunk with the star were arriving in England by S. S. *Alternative* * I would come scampering back from Greece, or from a whaling voyage in the Arctic, or from working as a stoker on the Harwich-Antwerp run, or from whatever other adventure which Europe was persistently offering to an irresponsible young American, and faithfully would I settle down to doing a fresh copy of the Book. Even after marriage, and the transition to office life (farewell to those long delicious aca-

* Perhaps this is too compressed a reference to one of Doctors' habits. In order to make quite sure of a passage he would make alternative bookings, and only toward the last moment, give up one in favour of the other.

demic holidays) the old routine persisted. It was sustained for a total of eleven years, by which time there were more than a thousand pages of foolscap manuscript, and diagrams beyond all numbering. In the summer of 1927 I finally remarked: " Now, Doctors, don't get me wrong. We're having a wonderful time, and we could go on forever, but if the idea is to publish this as a book, don't you think it is getting a little big?" At which he looked at me, and pulled his nose, and after a little reflection, answered: " You're perfectly right. There's too much of it. We'll have to cut."

That was a summer of much brooding, and toward the end he announced a method of cutting. We would reverse the procedure. For the winter he would leave the manuscript with me (Madame Doctors heard this announcement with a great bounce of joy) and I would go through it and mark the parts which I found easy to understand. " Then," said Doctors, " next summer we can strike out those parts. We want this to be a serious contribution." I got the point, and didn't disagree. The purpose of the Book had changed, along with its many transformations. It was now a new and original gift to the art of mathematics. There would be little point in putting forward for the astonishment of experts, what I myself could readily understand. Throughout that winter, with my wife's generous forbearance, and in the interstices of other labours, I made a number of marks on the manuscript, and the next summer we attended to the sutures.

For seven more years we pursued this new procedure. The thousand pages were now a mere two hundred. By dint of so much study I had mastered most of the material, and even began to have some qualms about the recalcitrant remnant. So on that seventh summer — the eighteenth from the beginning — once more I spoke: "Now, Doctors, don't get me wrong. If you leave the manuscript with me next winter, there's a chance I may understand all of it. Most certainly I'd be the better for that, but if the idea is to publish what I don't understand, don't you think it's already getting a little slim?" Doctors looked at me reflectively and said: "You're perfectly right. Anything less than what we have right now wouldn't make a Book. We'll publish."

The idea that there might be any difficulty about securing a publisher for the residue of his mathematics which I didn't happen to understand, never gained admittance to my father's head. Book-publishers, what do they exist for? (Sometimes I wonder.) Yet there wasn't too much difficulty, and for the next couple of years there was a happy to-ing and fro-ing of galley proofs and page proofs, a transaction which gives prodigious pleasure to all authors except the most jaded of that tribe. Came then the publication, and the reviews and considered acclamation of the dozen or so people scattered over the world whose opinions Doctors really valued — and then he died. I know that to each of his sons there remains a special sense of loss; yet we all recognize that both in the manner and the timing of his death he was fortunate. He was still "conspicuous for moderate habits and quiet industry." He had lost none of his power and none of his humor. In one romantic little final flutter with an oil well, he was still Captain Rosebud to the last. He had daddled the enemy, and not been busted. But he had reaped the harvest of all the patient labor on that particular Book, and was too old for further heavy harness or even for the Atlantic crossings which he so much enjoyed. His game had been well played throughout; and he was granted a good end.

But for a long while after Doctors' death I continued to be embarrassed about that Book. It carried my name as well as his, and though maybe I have exaggerated the story of its construction, it is true in the main that I was much more familiar with all that we discarded than with most of what stayed in. With Doctors alive, he had a merry time replying to correspondents who were excited about a result on page so-and-so. With Doctors dead, I found such questions very awkward. If only — I would groan — if only they would ask me questions about what isn't in the book, then I could stand examination.

As it was, I was pushed into all kinds of outward exertions in order to be obviously too busy to be expected to give a detailed reply. I had to erect some plausibility in order to state like Ruskin: " Mr. Morley has retired from correspondence." Finally I found the excuse in that fine phrase, Government Service.

I am now, as Polybius would say, in the exact middle of my meticulous analysis of the precise nature of chess.

An excuse, to be valid, must be true. However odd the fact might be, I was truly beginning to be temporarily embroiled in government service.

In 1939 I had returned from England to America, and what with a natural preoccupation with the course of war and the normal turmoil of the book-publishing game, it seems to me (quite apart from answering questions about Doctors' theorems) that those next years were tough. There were many gyrations of agony which I don't like to think of. But what is pertinent here is that in the course of some errand which had taken me to Washington, I happened to run into my old school-friend Burt Oppenheim, completely by accident, in the Washington Station restaurant. Burt is dead now, and I can say without his contradiction that he was a great man. What is the definition of greatness? Well, it is something quite apart from notoriety. It has nothing to do with winning votes in a popularity contest. A man can be in a manner divine and yet unknown to all. But it is also something not controlled by the possessor, but conferred upon him by those receptive to his spirit, by those who feel his restlessness for good, and who admit his power of trespass into their own closely-defended territory. It is something too which transcends death. A great man's good qualities go on. Burt, with his slightly-lopsided spiritual face, his squared up shoulders and his somewhat dragging walk, was at a glance a fellow whom medical men would know to have a bad heart, but the rest of mankind would know to have a good one. Even at school one could foretell that he might have the quality of greatness; in maturity, purged as he was by suffering, you could not fail to feel it. He was so much alive — alive to such a wide range of things; and he cared — he cared with an intensity which made you sit up and take notice, and possibly, though in a lesser way, begin to care a little too.

A dangerous, although delightful, accident, to run into Burt Oppenheim. Burt was a " traitor to his class " — a businessman, who was interested in labor-relations, and who resigned from business to spend the rest of his life, and actually to kill himself through over-work, as a minor civil servant. He was capable of higher office, but he didn't want high office. He had no personal ambition or any other vices through which you could get hold of him. He had no theories to prove, or desire to be the boss, or any vanity of any kind that I could ever discover, unless to expend one's self so fervently for simple things like fairness and efficiency in government be reckoned vanity. For those simple things he cared a lot; as I have said, he died for them; but in any given situation anybody less opinionated, or less " crack-pot," than Burt, I have yet to meet. And a dangerous fellow to meet, because he was in a position to recommend panel members for the public hearings called for under the United States Wage and Hours Act in labor-disputes in depressed industries. Nobody cares to be too much in the eye of the man who can pick you for jury-duty.

After the many years of separation, when we happened to have that chance meeting and had exchanged news, Burt suddenly cocked an eye at me and squared his shoulders and said, " Frank, I'm going to recommend you as a public member on one of these tripartite panels — we have to have members who represent industry, labor, and the public, and of course we have most difficulty in finding representatives of the public — and that's what I think you could do." I told Burt not to be ridiculous, that I had lived abroad for twenty years, that I was busy as a birddog with publishing activities, that I knew nothing whatever about government or labor relations and didn't want to learn. " No," said Burt, " that's not a right attitude in the first place; and in the second, so far as doing it, if you're a book-publisher you must be accustomed to dealing with difficult people, and that's the main part." " Don't be silly," said I, as we separated. " Don't be surprised," said Burt.

The first panel I served on was concerned with the knitted underwear industry. My business colleagues considered this a great joke, and in a spirit of hilarity voted me the necessary leave of absence. Immediately after Pearl Harbor the National War Labor Board was formed in Washington, and soon after that other panel hearings came very thick and very fast.

In full, the history of the National War Labor Board will never be written. The Board itself was a tripartite body of twelve men, with equal representation for industry, labor, and the public, set up by Executive Order of the President of the United States, and (in the beginning) with the sole duty of making a final determination of all labor disputes throughout the country by peaceable means. It had no power except persuasion. That is why the history will never be written. Persuasion — how can you describe it? It is the impress of character. Statistics won't reveal it. The verbal transcript, the famous " record " so faithfully kept by so many faithful recorders — I recall one occasion when the mere keeping of the record threw the recorder into an epileptic fit — that won't reveal it. In the beginning, I doubt if many people expected the War Labor Board, set up so loosely and in itself so powerless, to be able to function as a continuing and effective agency of government, in so tough and turbulent and undisciplined field as the field of labor disputes. It did function. That is why the history would be worth writing. Yet there is no science or art that I can think of which would make that history recordable.

The Board was a remarkable team of men, and a sufficiently remarkable team of remarkable men can do the impossible; but to say that does not explain it or describe it in detail. So much of the responsibility as any one man could carry should, I consider, be charged to Will Davis for the one central quality, beautifully identified in one of Lloyd Garrison's letters, in the words: " when Will Davis opens the door, faith enters with him." But no more than Burt Oppenheim, could Will Davis define that faith. All he could do was exemplify it. The lack of definition, of description, drove some people almost crazy; others it collected into the firmest kind of loyalty. As the phrase goes, I have been around; I have been places; I have seen occasions; but I have never seen a better team of better men in operation that that War Labor

Board team of Davis, Taylor, Graham, Garrison
. . . and so on, all the way along. In a democracy,
that last phrase is tremendously important: all the
way along. I've mentioned only public members.
The representatives of industry and labor were fully
as important and almost as remarkable. But none
of the representatives of industry and labor will pro-
test my greatest sympathy toward the members for
the public, because, in that set-up, their votes held
the balance of power. Where all the weights were
grievous, those of the public members were the heavi-
est. Where all the seats were hot, theirs were the
hottest.

I am speaking of the early days of the War Labor
Board in Washington, before there came along the
later and cumbersome duty of administering the
Wage Stabilization program, before the remarkable
biological fission (transcending that of the amoeba)
into Regional Boards — before all that. I am speaking of the days when, despite the fact that the Board
in Washington was supposed to be a sort of Supreme
Court in labor-relations rather than an instrument of
mediation, there was in actual practice quite a lot of
the human fun of mediating a dispute out of existence. That is what I need to refer to, and it will
show how anything in the nature of a history of the
War Labor Board is out of the question.

A labor dispute is composed of three ingredients
— heat, details, background — and so, to cool it off
and sort it out before it was brought to the Board
for a Board Order — after which it would be up to
everyone to tremble, whether the Order would be

obeyed — there would be a public hearing. Usually this was a full-dress business, not only the parties being present, but a full tripartite panel, with a panel assistant, recorders, reporters, and anybody else, if interested. Sometimes a public representative would find himself instructed to conduct a hearing as a single Hearings Officer; for this there were probably special reasons — no doubt, when all on my own I found myself hearing the troubles of the Chorus Ladies of America, somebody must have considered it unwise to expose too many people to such danger; and perhaps the same was true when without companions I heard the welders of an unnamed airplane factory, where members of rival unions had developed the habit of bopping each other on the head with hammers. But generally a hearing would be before a three-man panel. All parties would express their views; the panel would then struggle with the merits, and produce a written report and specific recommendations, unanimous or with strong dissents, as the case might be.

It was at this stage, when the disputants were present in person, that the human elements were uppermost, and there was a legitimate temptation for the chairman to obtain, if he could, an all-round agreement which would remove the case from the docket. The later stages of Review, Appeals, and, finally, Board Action, were all more abstract. In my experience of various positions with the Board the job of panel chairman, in the early days, was the most fun. You never knew what was going to turn up. In the little matter of the marine painters (the fellows who paint not seascapes but the actual ships) the lawyers on each side had been arguing technicalities with ten-dollar legal words for something like half an hour, before one of the shop-committee-men, one of the actual painters, leaped to his feet in indignation. He was a short, stout, very redfaced Scotsman, and it was his own lawyer whom he interrupted by banging his big fist on the table and shouting: " Mr. Chair-man, the trouble was, the snappers put shenangoes on the boot-tops." I hastily consulted the diagram of persons present, and made some such amiable, in-ane remark as, " Mr. Maxwell, I'm sure you have a point there if you'll explain it to us." Whereupon he banged his fist much more indignantly, and shouted much more angrily at me: " The trouble was, the snappers put shenangoes on the boot-tops! " I had the wit to let it pass, and presently to get the lawyers out of the room on the pretext of drafting some pre-amble, and by the time they returned we had ex-plored Mr. Maxwell's remarkable statement, and everything was removed from the docket, and hence-forth (so far as I know) more or less hunky-dory.*

Fun possibly is not the right word. It isn't alto-gether fun to hear both sides of a dispute and to have to take a decisive position. I know that repre-

* *Snappers*, my impression is, were a kind of under-foremen. *Shenangoes* were workers who were not regulars, but drifters; men who had hot feet, who would work for a few days in Brooklyn, and then drift to Philadelphia, Baltimore, Charleston, Dallas, San Fran-cisco or where-have-you. *Boot-tops* is the (presumably British) phrase for the paint below the water-line, where it changes color. *Hunky-dory* is when you can get a dispute effectively disposed of, and don't have to write a report or hear anything more about it.

sentatives of industry frequently felt that public members didn't know what they were doing, and didn't feel any compunction for their victims. I know that representatives of labor frequently acted as if public members should be an innocent, impressionable audience. It was possible to stand the cross-fire only if you were ready to make both sides really cross. Mr. Joseph Vance gave the infallible guide for arbitration: " Be as unfair as you can to 'em all! Make 'em swear at you, one same as t'other! In six weeks they'll be saying give me Wance for an Arbitrator!"

The office of a Mediator is differently defined. As stated by Lord Askwith, who knew what he was talking about, a Mediator has three qualities. The first is, patience; the second, patience; and the third — more patience.

All that a chairman of a National War Labor Board panel had to do in those early days was very simple — succeed or perish. That much was easy to understand. The rest was a little more difficult. What one was really called upon to exercise, without anybody knowing upon what authority, was judicial capacity, in a realm where there wasn't any law. I don't know how the other chairmen felt, for we were much too busy ever to see each other, but in many, many cases that I handled I was scared stiff. It might be a powder company, it might be surgical instruments; it might be the aircraft industry, or glass, or textiles, or furniture makers. It might be Insurance, it might be Laundries, it might be the Migratory Oil Drillers. It wasn't like an ordinary judicial career, because these were new problems, and there was no precedent whatever. Over these problems we would sit by day and often sit by night, sitting like frogs in the grottoes of the Department of Labor Building. Then, almost welcoming a state of utter loneliness, I would go back to the Willard Hotel; and yet, seeking some way out I would read over those rules drawn up for his private guidance by the great judge Sir Matthew Hale, and by him named *Things Necessary to be Continually Held in Remembrance:*

That I rest not on my own understanding or strength, but implore and rest upon the direction and strength of God.

That in the execution of judgment, I carefully lay aside my own passions, and not give way to them, however provoked.

That I be wholly intent upon the business I am about, remitting all cares and thoughts as unseasonable, and interruptions.

That I suffer not myself to be prepossessed with any judgment at all, 'till the whole business and both parties be heard.

That I be not too rigid in matters purely conscientious, where all the harm is diversity of judgment.

That I be not biassed with compassion to the poor, or favour to the rich, in point of justice.

That popular or court applause, or distaste, have no influence in point of distribution of justice.

Not to be solicitous what men will say or

think, so long as I keep myself exactly according to the rule of justice.

In criminals that consist merely in words, when no harm ensues, moderation is no injustice.

To abhor all private solicitations, of what kind soever, and by whomsoever, in matters depending.

To be short, and sparing, at meals, that I may be fitter for business.

I know nothing about Sir Matthew Hale except that memorandum, but I have often loved him for those private thoughts. I never succeeded in living up to all of his remembrances, but I did try, and I hope that in a human way he had his lapses too. With Matthew Hale in mind it was easier to present an imperturbable front to a sufficiently vicious quarrel, and at some stage get the sting out of it and if possible develop a little comedy, for if only the edge of hate and suspicion could be blunted by men laughing together, the chances for a settlement were better. When I say settlement, I don't necessarily mean compromise. I mean clarification. There's an old proverb, good fences make good neighbours. Most of these squabbles began by being fuzzy, and if both parties ran to their lawyers they got fuzzier and fuzzier. Joseph Vance was right. If you could get them both equally mad at Government, the chances were that they'd become friends and mutually clarify their own issues, and get back to work, and war production would go up. *That* was the over-all objective. Of course there were occasional failures. Out of the first three thousand dispute cases, the Board failed to settle seven. Failures continued in about the same proportion — in other words there were surprisingly few disputes which couldn't in some way or at some time be settled by persuasion. And not inconsiderable was the satisfaction of observing an Army or Navy award for increased output going to some company and union which, at the time when you knew them, had been spending their zeal in fighting each other.

A panel chairman who faced the physical contest between the parties themselves, was supported by the faith that if he made a mistake, the big Board itself, those twelve great men, in passing on his recommendation would alter or iron it out. A panel chairman would think of the Big Board as a sort of Ironing Board. That was true, yet it was also true that if a dispute got crumpled at the stage of the panel hearing, it was extremely troublesome later on to straighten it. So faith in the Big Board didn't decrease your desire to do your own ironing. In case after case, each with its own set of psychological peculiarities, that was good exercise.

Though I know many men who worked a great deal harder, the normal routine of those days was, for me, fairly active. On Monday the eight o'clock train would take me from Connecticut to New York for one day of publishing. I would stay at the New York office till midnight, then catch the bus for the B & O night train for Washington — there was a standing order for Lower Berth 5, Car No. 113. In

Washington I would breakfast at the Willard Hotel, and then the buzzle-wuzzle would begin. One could usually get back to Connecticut for a blessed Sunday with the family, so I don't claim undue hardship. The strain was to keep going in two intense, and completely separate, worlds.

As to the intensity of the work in labor disputes, I should like to refer to a case (not by name, though nobody who was concerned is likely to forget it) which opened on a Tuesday morning of such a routine week. It was a southern textile case, and it quickly appeared there was plenty of heat. Apart from a history of five strikes in two years, there were some thoroughly unpleasant episodes in the background, and the kind of bitter incompatibilities which you are likely to find with a management which is financially controlled from New England and an untamed labor force drawn from the Carolina hills. The Manager, as I shall call him, his lawyer, his expert in Personnel Relations, and other supporters were on one side of the table. Behind him, though far distant, you could perceive a board of directors, stockholders, and pressures none the less real because they were unrevealed. On the other side, the International Officer of the Union who was to be their spokesman, the local Union organiser, and the members of the Shop Committee, who were operatives from the mill itself, and who sat there, grim and thin-lipped, terribly intent to catch on to all that was about to happen. Behind them, though far distant, you could very clearly see the Carolina hills. Now the dispute was not about wages, which were being dealt with by a separate arbitrator. This dispute was over the negotiation of a first contract between the Company and the Union. They had so far never been able even to get started on a contract. That meant there were twenty-one issues on which the parties could or would reach no agreement whatever. It was obviously one of those cases in which everything had to be sewed up into a bundle, and the bundle accepted as a whole — or all the issues separately would fly out of the window.

I was particularly fortunate in the other panel members. For labor, there was Scotty Stewart; for industry, there was Henry Woodbridge. Could anybody doubt from the early pages of this narrative, that I should have a great affection for anyone named Woodbridge? Henry is worthy of the name. And Scotty — let me give you Scotty's quality. I recall an executive session of one of the Board's committees, when an industry member (not Woodbridge), goaded to exasperation, burst out with the remark: " Scotty, I *wish* you'd give me just a little consideration." Said Scotty instantly, in his delicious clipped, quick Glasgow accent, " I'll give you just as little as I can! " Scotty, like Alan Breck before him, is a bonny fighter and a fair one. Scotty and Woodbridge both respected each other, and both knew what it was all about, and if any pair of representatives could do so, they should have been able, by talking words of wisdom to their respective parties, to get the details sorted out, and balance this against that if need be, and sew up the desired bundle, and that would have been that.

That was very far from being that. Neither party wanted words of wisdom. Neither party wanted to do anything but fight — to fight as bitterly in Washington as in the mills of Carolina.

When people are really oblivious to every other consideration, and wish above all things to fight, I don't know what there is to do except, as I have suggested, to change the direction of the battle, and try to make them both fight you. That *may* turn them into allies. But whether it is proper or right or reasonable to change the direction of the battle, it isn't always easy. You have to feel your way. We started by writing down the issues, one by one to twenty-one, and attempted to get into parallel columns what the Company would agree to and what the Union; but of course on the first day nobody agrees to anything; each side wants to accuse and convict the other, and blow off steam. You don't throttle anybody; you'll get nowhere till that steam has blown off, and far from cutting it short, you make quite sure that they are exhausted. You make quite sure that the visit to Washington isn't just a joy-ride. We had a recess for lunch, but without any recess for dinner we sat that first night till after eleven o'clock. On Wednesday we started once again with the issues; once again the steam was blown; and Wednesday night without recess for dinner we sat on till two in the morning. The reason I stayed at the Willard is that it is very handy to the Department of Labor; you can walk to your bed in a couple of minutes.

I may say it is very important for a chairman at such sessions to have sufficient physical self-control never to have to leave the conference room. So long as the parties are suspicious of each other, they won't leave either. By Thursday evening, with the same routine apparently obtaining, I noticed that they both were begining to glare at me, instead of glaring exclusively at each other. This War Labor Board excursion seemed to them a lot more tedious than the life to which they were accustomed. I was somewhat assisted by Scotty Stewart and Henry Woodbridge barking at me too, and also the panel assistant, for they had all had hopes of a weekend. That very same Thursday night the first agreement was reached, on one of the inconsequential issues — conditional, of course, on the fantastic hypothesis that satisfactory agreement could be reached on all the others. That's where Scotty and Woodbridge came to my aid in making it clear that *we* weren't making the agreement for the parties. If they brought us their agreement, made on all issues and to be kept in good faith, we would consider it, and if they both wanted it, we would recommend it to the Board. I forget what time we broke up Thursday night, but it was after midnight.

On the Friday morning, as I was ambling to our little session, the Manager (for the Company) caught me in the corridor, and said, with real tears in his eyes: " Mr. Morley, in that clause we agreed to last night there were some words inserted by the Union. Mr. Morley, it has always been my deepest principle that *words* are the *prerogative* of *Management*."

By Friday evening we had really made some progress. Fifteen or sixteen issues were tentatively agreed, and the panel was not suggesting but resisting, and only gradually over-powered by the desire of the parties to find clauses (including mutually discovered words) that were mutually acceptable. I made a bold experiment. We recessed for two hours for dinner — and came back to clean up all except the two or three really tough issues which remained.

Saturday, on the War Labor Board in Washington, was always quite a day. Many people would have endeavoured to make reservations to get home, and as the clock neared each respective deadline, each escapist was apt to get panicky. As Matthew Hale might have said, that's not a thing which ought to influence your judgment. Scotty was all right; he had altered his plans and was remaining in Washington. Henry Woodbridge and I (through the good graces and unforgettable help of Thelma Merrill) had reservations on the nine o'clock plane for New York — nine o'clock P.M., which on Saturday morning seemed a fair enough bet. But we underestimated the whiplash of those fighters. All day Saturday there was squabbling on the final issues. What a waste of time it seemed! But it was *their* collective bargaining, their free right to do it the hard or easy way. The panel was there as a catalytic agent, to persuade if possible; if not, to make recommendations to the Board.

By Saturday afternoon, on account of disagreement on the final issues, we had gone right back to nowhere. About four o'clock I thought we would call a halt and recess till seven. I wanted Stewart and Woodbridge to talk with the respective parties, and give me their final opinions at the Willard. While I waited for them, I was reduced to reading the copy of the Bible supplied to each hotel room by the indefatigable Society of Gideons.

As to any complete and final agreement, the report from Woodbridge, the report from Stewart, was completely negative. The thing had blown up on us, that was all there was to it. A week was all that we'd wasted, but twenty-one unresolved issues would occupy the Big Board more than that. It wasn't just a silly little case; it had some key importance. And Henry and Scotty, with the parties in disagreement, were of course relieved from any necessity of assent to the Chairman's report, which I would have to write. A rotten thing to send to the Board, crumpled and torn three ways.

When we resumed at seven with the parties, I said I would read them a sermon consisting of three parts of three texts copied from a book worthy of attention. I read the words:

Romans XV 5   "Now the God of patience and consolation grant you to be likeminded one toward another. . . ."

I Corinthians VII 9 . ". . . it is better to marry than to burn."

I Corinthians VII 15 " But if the unbelieving depart, let him depart. . . ."

[77]

For those particular contestants it chanced to do the trick. St. Paul and the hour provided the catalysis. Both parties signed a petition for complete agreement on twenty issues, and the objection on the remaining one was pro forma. The case was removed from the docket, and Henry and I caught the nine o'clock plane.

That wasn't typical. Nothing about those hearings was typical, except that they were exhausting. It was on another night than that, when something really had blown up, and everything was jargled, and Henry Woodbridge was attempting to revive me at his hotel (The Carlton), that I at last said: " Henry, unless we can play a game of chess, I think I shall go completely nuts."

The point of this long story is that under some pressures, some men may actually need chess; and need it, not just to beat or to be beaten, but as a dromenon. This need is much more than a craving for any mere narcotic. It is a creative reaction to an irrational environment, to assert a revival of orderliness; it is a reaction against the darkness which is darkness itself, without any order; and a reaction not just by yourself, in isolation, but in a confident companionship.

At any rate, that's how chess came to the National War Labor Board, and the fever was revived in many other players, and it expanded the human contacts, and was altogether healthy.

10

The Master said, Are there not games played on boards?
To play them would surely be better than doing nothing at
all. . . .

Analects of Confucius, Book XVII

I CAN now expose the reason for a proposed change
in the chessboard.

So far I hope I haven't seemed too backward-
looking. I intended to recoil in order to spring upon
the future. I used the example of chess with my father as an illustration. But I am more concerned
about chess with my children. In the middle of the
journey of our life that becomes an important question.

Nowadays there are ubiquitous complications. In
Colonel William C. Menninger's paper on *The Men-
tally or Emotionally Handicapped Veteran* I read
that: " Forty-eight per cent of the discharges for dis-
ability between January and June 1944 were on the
basis of neuro-psychiatric disorders. . . . The family . . . should aid in increasing the number of family-shared experiences; it should make the present
rich with understanding and unquestioning companionship. . . ." * In the same issue of the same jour-

* *The Annals of the American Academy of Political and Social
Science*, Vol. 239, May 1945, pp. 23, 27.

nal I read the advice of Dr. Norman Cameron:
" Provide the veteran with recreational facilities and
vitally necessary social opportunities. It would be a
serious mistake to look upon all this as mere idle entertainment or escape. . . ."

I take it that what the doctors are saying is that
the treatment for war-veterans, is the same treatment
that is valid for the rest of human beings who have
been under special pressures and who, because of time
spent otherwise, may be at a disadvantage in a usable
kind of learning. To a layman that would seem to
be common sense. War-veterans are not the only
ones to make adjustments. Adjustments must be
made by all. And adjustment, to any human being,
involves strain.

The proponents of chess have always been modest
in their statements about its therapeutic value. The
loveliest poetry makes almost irresistible the music
of Despair:

> Is not short paine well borne, that brings long ease,
> And layes the soule to sleepe in quiet grave?
> Sleepe after toyle, port after stormie seas,
> Ease after warre, death after life does greatly please.

As against that, what can you find for the weak and
odd and puny case — and yet a positive case — which
I am trying to make out? How sardonic is the mild
encouragement of the Master whom I have quoted
at the beginning of this section: " Are there not games
played on boards? To play them would surely be
better than doing nothing at all. . . ." How gentle
is the claim of that Chess-Master, Emanuel Lasker:
" And chess may do its little share. . . ."

Of course the proponents of chess are right to be modest. How few people there are who think of it as a means of conversation, as a therapy. Yet, of the available instruments, it is much easier to come by than the piano, which Beethoven used when he wanted to talk, or than the gift which Leonardo had, of talking into his notebooks. Chess is just about the easiest of the interest-paying dromenons. That is what I have been trying to exemplify. I have tried to show how under his particular pressures my father found " understanding and unquestioning companionship " at chess; how he found " social opportunities "; how in his life it would indeed be as Dr. Cameron says, " a serious mistake to look upon all this as mere idle entertainment or escape." Even for those who are not " natural " players, there are times when chess is needed.

Yet I have also admitted that chess, of its nature, is imperfect for any pair of players who are separated by a disparity of power or of learning. An intuition I am proud of was that when I *needed* chess, I picked upon Henry Woodbridge; for I had no foreknowledge that Henry's grandfather had played Steinitz to a draw, and that Henry and I were in the same stage of degeneration.

For I, even I, a fourth-class player (or in my highest flights of self-esteem a third) am caught in the social trap set up by the ancient board. I, even I, have learned too much to play chess with some beginners with whom I should like to play. I, even I, who know so little, am unable to play down to those who know still less.

What I am talking about is the normal curtain which bars " unquestioning companionship " between two generations, unless there can be found a mutual conversation, a mutual dromenon. What I am talking about is the chasm which peculiarly separates men who have " lost time " in the war and their relatives at home. What do you do to bridge that chasm? When they get back, how do you re-establish communication? What devices of companionship are there in common? What are your means of following Colonel Menninger's advice, of " increasing the number of family-shared experiences? " If after separation you have the chance of being together, and want to relax and decelerate, how do you do so?

Of course you and your son might go fishing, or both together write a book of mathematics. But the younger of you might suggest a game of chess.

If that should happen, wouldn't it be more merciful toward the purpose of having mutual fun if, without an overt handicap, there could be an equality of intercourse?

Leaving out all decoration, my argument is simply this. If you want to arrange an equality of intercourse over the chessboard what you have to do is to remove from the mind of one player or add to the mind of the other, the surplus or deficiency of previous study of the game. Only thus can you have the generous excitement of comparing sheer tactical skills.

You need a surgical operation.

On what do you need to operate? Not the players, not the chessmen. Nor do you tamper with the rules of the game, with the established dromenon. The reason for that is as old as Plato: " Gods and temples are not easily instituted, and to establish them rightly is the work of a mighty intellect." * The players' minds you cannot touch, the chessmen and the rules (unless you claim to have a mighty intellect) you should not touch. On what do you operate?

You operate on the chessboard. It is the old square chessboard which is played out, not as among equals, but as among unequal players. It is the square chessboard which, not of itself but because of the excessive study it has received, implants the rigid class-distinctions upon chess — distinctions which the players can't of themselves surmount.

Even a moderate intellect may suggest surgical operations to be performed on the board.

* *Laws* X 909.

11

DEMOSTHENES: My poor old mate, how d'ye feel?
NICIAS: Bad, as bad as you do.

Aristophanes *Knights* (translated by J. M. Edmonds)

I WAS about to say that there was nothing new about the idea of such a surgical operation, when who should crop up again, and on my side, but Old Bird!

If you care to obtain *The City of London Chess Magazine* for June, 1874 (Price Sixpence), you will find the following article under the great signature of H. E. BIRD. I print it nearly in extenso.

A PROPOSED MODIFICATION IN THE GAME OF CHESS

" The game of chess has so long occupied the foremost place amongst amusements of an intellectual character, that any proposal to introduce a variation therein may, not unnaturally, be received, at its first announcement, with some degree of astonishment, if not with positive dissatisfaction; feeling this, I have, before venturing to give publicity to my own views, taken the precaution of conferring with some leading Chess amateurs on the subject, the result being that two or three of us have arrived at the conclusion that a trifling modification of the Chess board and pieces, not tending to trench upon the general principles of the game, would be worthy of consideration. It has

[84]

been suggested that a trial should be made to test the practical working of the game with the board and men as now submitted. With this end in view, a short match will probably be arranged between two leading players, when it is thought that by publishing the best games, an opportunity will be afforded to those who take sufficient interest in the matter to offer any opinions that may suggest themselves in regard thereto. It is needless to add that hints, calculated to promote the interest in the noble game, will be most welcome, and, without wishing to attach undue importance to any amusement, it may safely be assumed that anything tending to popularize the most innocent and scientific of all sedentary recreations will be considered worthy of countenance by nearly all classes.

" In a few words, the reason which may be said to exist for rendering a slight modification of the game desirable, seems to be as follows :

" Chess, having now been played in its present form for nearly four hundred years, has been analysed to such an extraordinary extent that the openings have become almost stereotyped, and exercise so great an influence on the conduct of the game as to place the amateur not acquainted with them at a great disadvantage. The knowledge which can be acquired by a study of the multitude of works on Chess Openings confers such an immense advantage on the well-read player that the young Chess aspirant is often completely routed before the game arrives at its most interesting stage, and he becomes discouraged, sometimes attributing his want of success to his own inaptitude for the game, when, in reality, it may arise from his not having had leisure or opportunity to acquire an acquaintance with the opening sufficient to launch him fairly into the game.

"It has been found, upon examination, that the addition of two Pawns to the board would, without affecting the principle of the game, add greatly to the number of eligible openings, and afford full scope to the original player, who relies mainly on his own resources and powers of combination. Book knowledge would be of much less avail than at present, and the infusion of novelty . . . would, I believe, add greatly to the popularity of the game.

"The addition of the two Pawns on the same line where the eight Pawns are at present placed, necessarily involves a widening of the board to ten squares instead of eight squares, the length of the board remaining as at present, but the King and Queen will, of course, stand upon different colours than heretofore. . . . Two blank squares [Mr. Bird refers to the two squares in the back row of his eight by ten board, which are on either side of the King and Queen] remain to be filled up, and as to the name, form and powers of the two pieces to be placed thereon, some diversity of opinion may reasonably be expected. It is proposed that one placed by the side of the Queen, be called the Guard, and the other, by the side of the King, the Equerry; the first, in form of Rook and Knight, may be played as either at any move of the game; the other, in form of Bishop and Knight, may be played as either at any move of the game. In case it should be found in practice that

[86]

the two new pieces on each side form too great an addition to the power of the forces, I have selected, as an alternative proposition, a board nine squares wide, by eight long, with only one Pawn added, and one additional piece in form of Rook and Pawn, combining at each move the powers of both.

" I have reason to believe that sufficient interest will be felt in the proposed modifications to ensure their being tested in actual play, and admirers of Chess will, it is hoped, combine to endeavour to preserve the game in the position which it has so long occupied. The waning popularity of Chess during the years 1871 and 1872 engendered the fear, with some, that, as a leading amusement for places of public resort, it would die out, and be supplanted by some other of a more exciting character. The fact that the Westminster Chess Club, originally formed, as its name denotes, for the purpose of Chess, became converted, in the course of three years, completely into a Whist club, is sufficiently ominous. . . ."

Good Mr. Bird! I cannot quote the old warhorse without affectionate admiration. But let's not underestimate the staying-power of chess on the ancient chessboard. It survived the defection of the fainthearted Westminster members, as it had survived the slump of 1871 and 1872. It has survived Bird's fears, and the fears of every Master since who has felt that it was getting played out. As soon as one Master claims that the game is exhausted, another Master is likely to arise and oust him. There is no reason why the ancient game on the ancient board should not last forever. My argument has never been against it — as a game for players of approximate equality, equality of natural power and equality of study. I welcome the support of the Masters when they talk about alterations not from any fear or desire that the old game should go out, but as evidence that it is not unpractical to think about alterations which may give unequal and unlearned players more of a chance.

Bird's suggested chessboard of ten by eight squares didn't catch on. Capablanca, as I have mentioned, endorsed it in principle, but even then I don't recall that it got beyond the stage of discussion and newspaper interviews.

Perhaps, by introducing extra pieces, these Masters aimed too high? Apart from other considerations, few private players are going to go to the trouble of obtaining an enlarged set of chessmen. There is something almost irreverent in that thought. Many people may be stimulated to dig out the once familiar chessmen which (whether or no in a red and white striped bag with a draw-string) are somewhere about the house — or, if not, a traditional set is not too hard to obtain. But an enlarged set of chessmen, with new pieces and new moves, seems very formidable. Such further complication might be fun for experts, but for the feeble folk for whom I'm speaking — the spider, the conies, and the grasshopper — such a cure is worse than the disease.

12

And games being, at least in intent, a remodelling of Life
— simplified, to be sure, but still resembling it in essentials
— there has to be an analogy between games and Life.

Emanuel Lasker, *Manual of Chess*

EVERYTHING so far reinforces the instinct that the surgical operation should be performed upon the chessboard only; and, furthermore, that a minor operation, if performed in time, may be better than a major one.

There is, of course, not merely one way, but many, in which surgery may be applied to the ancient chessboard. I have to confess that the particular suggestion illustrated in Figure 2 arose in fact before all the notions subsequently expressed were so laboriously strung together. The suggestion arose at a Directors' Meeting, and the line of thought was not so much a line of thought as a line of doodling.

I was ruminating that though we all piously pretend that everybody ought to have equality of opportunity, the stiff pattern of nature as well as of society is always cramping the individuals who are crowded to the fringes; and, as I had been sketching squares on the paper in front of me, I began to think how the apparently free and equal set-up of chessmen on the symmetrical board of eight by eight squares was nevertheless unfair to the two Rook's Pawns on either side. All the Rook's Pawns had opportunity to do, was to scrape forward alongside a blank wall. Each other Pawn could at once strike out to right or left, if occasion should arise; but the Rook's Pawns were all the time one-sided. Like the plaice I used to fish for off Nantucket, if they wanted to see anything of the game they were playing in, they would have to move both eyes to the one side of their head.*

There, thought I (for there was nothing much else to think about at the Directors' Meeting) — there was discrimination for you! Not intentional, of course. Nothing apparently more even-handed could be devised than a square chessboard. Yet there was this discrimination. A fine rage at this mistreatment of the Rook's Pawns caused me to sketch the outside corridors. The idea was, fair play for Pawns. Admittedly, this provision of fair play involved each Rook's Pawn in a new risk. If by capturing a piece a Rook's Pawn got into the corridor, he might never get back to the Rook's file, and so never have a chance of becoming a Queen, unless by capturing something else he could return to the full field of play. But I felt the Pawn himself should be the judge of that risk. There ought to be free will. He ought to make his own choice. He ought not to be precluded by the board itself from taking his chances.

The notation of the squares of the two corridors

* "In the old days with a galling basket on my shoulders I used to carry fish from Argos to Tegea. . . ." Simonides, quoted by Aristotle, *Rhetoric*, 1. 7. 1365a. Or perhaps this footnote is misplaced, and should refer to a later period?

presents no difficulty. The conventional chess notation (Figure 4) reckons each player's moves from

| 8 | 7 | 6 | 5 | 4 | 3 | 2 | 1 |

QRC QR QKt QB Q K KB KKt KR KRC

FIGURE 4

his own side of the board, White always at the bo
tom of the diagram, Black always at the top. Fo.
example White calls the squares along his Queen's
Rook's file, from the bottom to the top of the diagram, Q R 1, Q R 2, . . . Q R 8 respectively. It
is analogous to identify the squares in the Queen's
Rook's Corridor as Q R C 2, Q R C 3, . . . Q R C 7.
Similarly, White's King's Rook's Corridor may be
numbered (from the bottom of the diagram to the
top) as K R C 2, K R C 3, . . . K R C 7. The
squares Q R C 2 and K R C 2 are of interest. They
are not necessary for the alledged purpose of giving
fair play to White's Pawns (though Q R C 7 and
K R C 7 may be needed for that purpose) but I had
already begun to think about the Knights. When

[91]

the men are set up it is important that every square within the first three rows should be guarded. Although Q R C 2 and K R C 2 look naked, they are guarded by the respective Knights; and also, being vacant, they give the Knights another possible opening move. That is one of the functions of a Knight, to be able to open things up. On the other hand, according to my fancy it would never do to have corner squares, because if they were filled it would mean extra pieces, and if they were unfilled it would alter the discipline and perhaps spoil the character of the Rooks. Therefore Q R C 1, K R C 1 and consequently Q R C 8 and K R C 8 are conspicuously absent from Figures 2 and 4.

I had got as far as that when the Directors' Meeting became unduly personal, but the idle doodling had made a sufficient impression for me to sketch out a full-size board with corridors when I had a chance to do so, and from a number of trial games which have been played the possibilities I have claimed for it seem to be — possibilities.

A first question is, how much change is actually effected by the existence of the corridors. There are two answers, psychological and technical. In the psychological department, some players will be disposed to be experimental and to try completely different openings. This leads to new situations appearing right away. Others will tend to stick to familiar beginnings and utilize the extra space of the corridors only as a last (but perhaps very welcome) resort. If you play for adventure you will find plenty of difference. If you prefer to be conventional the corridors may be almost unused. But whether in any given game their effect is much or little, they provide a potential which, without being overwhelming, is sufficient to create new interest.

If I were competent to analyze the full effect of the corridors (which I am not) I would be the last person to do so. My purpose is only to say that between the stodgiest of players new alternatives will keep arising on the board with corridors, to the advantage of the man who can make better use of them. It is not my purpose to say more than that. It is obvious that when an attack is so poised that it may sweep from side to side, the added width of the board enhances the scope and the drama. It is obvious that the Bishops and the Rooks may tangle somewhat earlier. It is obvious that the question whether or not to castle, calls for re-examination. It is obvious that the threat of trapping a Rook's Pawn in a corridor from which he may never be able to escape leads to some new end-game complications. Yet it would defeat the whole intent which I have stated so elaborately if all the possibilities of the new board were too rapidly studied and learned — if the corridor board were too rapidly taped. On the other hand, unless I produce some examples it won't seem very real.

As a first example I will take the game already quoted between Mr. Bird and my father. Suppose that game were being played on a board with corridors. Between players who wished to stick to the old openings the first 8 moves might well have been the same. On the 9th move of the game as previously quoted (p. 25), White pushed his King's Knight's Pawn to K Kt 3 in order to harry the Black Queen. In that actual game the Black Queen went to (Black's) Kt 5. This was then the position:

FIGURE 3 (repeated).

From her previous position at KR 5, where else could the Black Queen go? There is no available counter-attack. Go she must. Four possible places were all she had to go to, K R 3, K R 4, Kt 4, Kt 5. She would be cramped at K R 3, though, since she would there be free from immediate attack that move might enable the Black King to Castle, and, after White's move B — K 2 (had that still taken place) the Black Queen might have gone to K R 6, or even Kt 4. As the event proved, Black's Q — K R 3 couldn't have been worse than the text move. But it was scarcely attractive, and on any other of the three squares to which the Black Queen might move she is subject to pressure which forces her to move again while White's position steadily strengthens. On the ancient board, Bird at his 9th move was in serious trouble.

Suppose that game were being played on a board with corridors? Figure 3 is then replaced by a new diagram (Figure 5). As an alternative for Black,

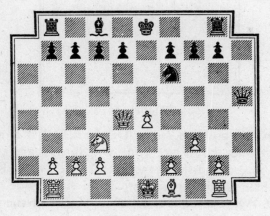

FIGURE 5

Figure 5 shows another possible 9th move, namely, Q — K R C 4. Whether that is or is not a good move I must leave to more competent analysts. It is at least another possibility, with no book to show that it is fatal.

Another example I find in one of Philidor's analyses of simple endings. With superb appreciation, this ending (Figure 6) is discussed in Lasker's *Manual of Chess*, pp. 202–204. The comments in quotation marks are not from me but from Emanuel Lasker.

[95]

FIGURE 6

"In this position," says Dr. Lasker, "it is note-worthy that the White King and Bishop are excel-lently placed and that consequently the White Rook is enabled to threaten Mate from either side. Of course, White will not allow Black to disturb the posi-tion of the White King, hence, the first move is a Check to tie up the Rook."

1. R — B 8 ch.   R — Q 1
2. R — B 7   ....

"threatening R — K R 7."

2. ....   R — Q 7

"The following point in Philidor's analysis is deep. The Black Rook is forced to leave [White's] second row, and forced on to the third row. There the Bishop and King will be able to exert a stronger pres-sure upon the Rook than if it stood further distant."

3. R — Q R 7		R — Q 8
4. R — K Kt 7		R — K B 8
5. B — Kt 3 !		. . . .

" The Bishop guards K square and thus prevents Check; it also prevents the Rook from returning to the second row."

5.		R — B 6

" With the Rook on the third row comes an inter-lude. The Bishop returns without losing any time."

6. B — Q 6		R — K 6 ch.
7. B — K 5		R — B 6

" Again another episode; the White Rook, with-out losing a move, goes to K Kt 4."

8. R — K 7 ch.		K — B 1
9. R — Q R 7		K — Kt 1
10. R — K Kt 7 ch.		K — B 1
11. R — K Kt 4		K — K 1

" And now all is prepared for the winning coup."

12. B — B 4		. . . .

" The Bishop dominates K 3 and thus prevents the saving Check; it also obstructs the Rook; all is at an end."

This " lovely main-play," as Lasker calls it might take place without alteration on the corridor board; I have put it in as ground-bait to attract attention to Philidor's two fine variations. In each case, after following the play on the ancient board, as recorded by Lasker and with his comments in quotation marks,

I want to see what difference is made by the existence of the corridors.

The first variation in the above play begins at the 5th move.

5.	K — B 1
6. R — Kt 4	K — K 1
7. R — Q B 4	R — Q 8

" or 7. K — B 1; 8. B — K 5, K — Kt 1; 9. R — K R 4."

8. B — R 4	K — B 1
9. B — B 6	R — K 8 ch.
10. B — K 5	K — Kt 1
11. R — K R 4	

Here is the position at the beginning of the above variation, but set up this time on the corridor board:

Position after White's 5th move.

FIGURE 7

If in this position the Black King moves to his Bishop's square, it seemed to me at first sight that the

[98]

Bishop would provide an immediate quietus by moving to K R C 5. Aha! thought I — after that fine move into the corridor all will be gas and gaiters. A splendid example wherein the existence of the corridor completely eliminates the variation! But a more sober thought prevails, because after White plays B — K R C 5 Black can retort with R — K 8 check. White cannot play B × R because then the Black King captures the White Rook and the game is drawn. If after Black plays R — K 8 check, White moves K — Q 6, then Black checks again until he forces the White King away from the square K 6 or Q 6 so that he can then play K — K 1, and thus escape the immediate threat of the discovered check. So by that tempting move the Bishop merely over-reaches himself, and, though not devoid of interest, it is not what I was looking for, a striking demonstration of the difference effected by use of the corridor.

However, if the first variation fails to provide me with a satisfactory example, I breathe again because a second variation does so. This variation begins after White's 4th move in the above main-play. Here Lasker points out that " the circumstance of the Chess-board's having only eight, and not nine, lines is made use of to catch the Black Rook, the Black King being unable to fly on to an (imaginary) ninth line." On the ancient board, this is how it runs :

4.	K — B 1
5. R — K R 7	R — K Kt 8
6. R — Q B 7	K — Kt 1
7. R — B 8 ch.	K — R 2
8. R — R 8 ch.	

" If the Chess-board extended further," Lasker comments, " Black could save himself and the ending would be a Draw. As it is, the Rook is lost." This is a very pretty example of the difference provided by the corridor board; for on that chessboard the Black King does escape into his Rook's Corridor, and is thankful.

This example seems to me sufficient for my purpose. I hope ingenious analysts may be persuaded to provide others.*

I know from trial that the new board provides a very good game,† and that though the better chess-

* After this was in proof I had an opportunity of showing the corridor board to Harold M. Phillips, and that veteran chess master did not dismiss it, but took an immediate kindly interest. He thought " the idea worthy of further exploration as a novel contest between friends who do not care to follow the routine of much-analyzed chess openings." He was at once struck with the question whether one could force mate on the corridor board with a King and two Bishops against a lone King, or with a King, Bishop and Knight against a lone King. Offhand, his expectation was that mate can be forced by King and two Bishops against a lone King, but not by King, Bishop and Knight. He suggested that if further analysis proves that to be so, the difficulty could be overcome by making it a rule that a King may not at any time move into the corridor.

Mr. Phillips also pointed out that in positions where a lone King will draw against the adverse King and Pawn on the old board, he will still draw against King and every Pawn on the new board, except against a Pawn on the Rook's file. He envisaged other interesting variants in the play, which he considered worthy of further study.

† The reader might wish to know how the relative powers of the chess-pieces on the corridor board compare with their relative powers on the old board. W. W. Rouse Ball, in his *Mathematical Recreations and Essays* (Macmillan, 5th Edition, 1911, p. 110 ff.) discusses the estimates from practice and from theory for the square chessboard. Two estimates from practice are as follows:

player will always win, the control of the game depends upon tactical ability rather than upon the book. So the new board does to some extent reduce class-barriers. But a word of caution to the innocent. If hitherto your consolation for being beaten resided in blaming the other fellow's book-knowledge, any challenge you make on the new board will put that consolation to the touch!

Old Board	Rook	Knight	Bishop	Queen
Staunton:	4 1/2	2 1/2	3	8 1/4
Von Bilguer:	4 1/2	3	3	8 1/4

A theoretical test used by Rouse Ball is to estimate the value of a piece by the chance that when it and a King are put at random on the board, it may take the King without giving the King an opportunity of taking it. Rouse Ball calls this a method of estimating values by " safe check." The calculation, which is quite easy, leads to this scale:

Old Board	Rook	Knight	Bishop	Queen
Safe Check:	5 2/3	2 2/3	3	8 2/3

This scale, computed theoretically on the criterion of the chance of a safe check, may be compared with the above estimates from practice. It will be borne in mind that all that is being computed, in this theoretical scale, is the unimpeded power of the pieces on a board deserted by all others except a defenceless King — a situation never reached in actual play, because, in play, both Kings are always present. But since I cannot produce sufficient practical evidence to make an estimate of the relative powers of the pieces on the corridor board, all I can do is to calculate a scale by safe check:

New Board	Rook	Knight	Bishop	Queen
Safe Check:	5 1/5	2 1/2	2 9/10	8 1/10

There is not a great deal of difference in these theoretical scales. Perhaps one may draw the deduction that there would not be a great deal of difference in the scales established by practice.

Of course, on either board, such relative values are only true " by and large." At all moments of actual play the values vary according to the position.

13

I am one of those knights of whom people tell, who go in
quest of adventures. . . .

Don Quixote, Part II, Chapter XVI

LOOKING into W. W. Rouse Ball's delightful book,
as the last footnote caused me to do, has also reminded me of the classic problem of moving a piece
over the chessboard in such a way that it shall suc-
cessively visit every square once and only once. In
particular it is the Knight's tour around the chessboard which can always arouse interest. The old
board has been thoroughly mastered.* Can he do

* " The literature on this subject is so extensive," says Rouse Ball,
" that I make no attempt to give a full account of the various methods
for solving the problem." For a bibliography he refers to A. van der
Linde, *Geschichte und Literatur des Schachspiels*, Berlin, 1874, vol.
II, pp. 101–111; to P. Volpicelli in *Atti della Reale Accademia dei
Lincei*, Rome, 1872, vol. XXV, pp. 87–162; also *Applications de
l'Analyse Mathématique au Jeu des Échecs*, by C. F. de Jaenisch, 3
vols., St. Petersburg, 1862–3; and General Parmentier, *Association
Française pour l'avancement des Sciences*, 1891, 1892, 1894.

Rouse Ball also refers to De Moivre, Euler, Vandermonde, Warns-
dorff and Roget. The specific reference to Euler (whose method I
am about to adopt) is to the *Mémoires de Berlin* for 1759, Berlin,
1766, pp. 310–337, and *Commentationes Arithmeticae Collectae*, St.
Petersburg, 1849, vol. I, pp. 337–355.

I ought to add that the reference to W. W. Rouse Ball, *op. cit.*, is
to pp. 122–132. That is the only reference I have looked up, so I
wouldn't dare to claim that what I intend to do hasn't been done
before. It almost certainly has been done, if not by Euler, at least
by T. Ciccolini, *Del Cavallo degli Scacchi*, Paris, 1836.

the same trick on the new board, and scamper around the whole pasture?

The answer is, of course he can, if he follows a right procedure.* For example:

	71	60	73	56	9	12	53	50	
59	74	57	10	13	54	49	36	39	52
70	61	72	55	8	11	22	51	48	37
75	58	69	62	23	14	7	38	35	40
68	63	66	25	6	21	34	41	30	47
65	76	3	18	15	24	27	44	33	42
2	67	64	5	26	17	20	29	46	31
	4	1	16	19	28	45	32	43	

FIGURE 8

This figure shows a complete re-entrant path for the Knight's tour on the corridor board. The corridor board has a total of 76 squares. Supposing that the Knight starts from his traditional position (the square numbered 1) the figure shows a sequence of moves by which he visits each square once and only once, and by which the 76th move brings him back, so that he can start all over again.

There is nothing particularly unexpected in the observation that the Knight can make a re-entrant tour

* To find out that procedure, as I have said in the previous footnote, I follow Euler's method. Yet out of gentility I am not putting the whole argument into the text, nor even into a footnote, but into a little Appendix, which I shall call a Pendant, where the curious may improve upon it, but nobody else need bother.

around the corridor board just as readily as he can around the ancient chessboard. Well-tried methods of travel apply to boards of many shapes other than square. Suppose, for instance, that to the corridor board so far described, which in the diagrams has been pictured with vertical corridors at the right and left, there were added two new horizontal corridors at the top and bottom. You would then have the shape shown in Figure 9, which has a total of 88

		25	22	79	28	73	76		
	23	14	27	82	75	78	29	72	
13	26	11	24	21	80	83	74	77	58
10	15	86	81	84	33	40	59	30	71
87	12	9	20	39	36	31	34	57	60
8	19	16	85	32	41	38	61	70	55
17	88	3	42	37	44	35	56	67	62
2	7	18	5	50	47	66	63	54	69
	4	1	48	43	52	45	68	65	
		6	51	46	49	64	53		

FIGURE 9

squares, and the figure shows how the Knight may make a complete re-entrant tour of that new shape.

By introducing Figure 9 I may have repeated a mistake made previously by Old Bird.

14

" Another game? " he asked.

" Naturally," answered Dr. B. with an enthusiasm that was disturbing to me. . . .

Stefan Zweig, *The Royal Game* (translated by B. W. Huebsch)

WHEN I ran across Old Bird's " proposed modification " in *The City of London Chess Magazine* I felt he had made a mistake in ever mentioning " an alternative proposition."

I have just made that same mistake. That " shape " just seen in Figure 9 is still another chessboard:

FIGURE 10

The weakness of presenting alternative proposals is that it looks as if the fellow who presents them hasn't made up his mind. He won't face a final decision. He wants a way out.

Before answering that, let me say there are many different minds to be made up. To some people the first corridor board (Figure 2) is a fearsome revolution. To others it is certain to seem not revolutionary enough. All that I am suggesting is that the double corridor board (Figure 10) is a possible second derivative for those to whom the first is not a sufficient novelty.

In the game as played on the double corridor board, everything in the way of rules and conventions is still the same, but there is the amusing prospect of getting around behind your opponent, or there is his alternative device of a defence in depth. I hold no brief for Figure 10, unless it should interest someone with whom you want to play, and serve, better than the other boards, to produce a better game.

The surgical operation doesn't matter, the change of boards doesn't matter — *which* operation, *which* change — doesn't matter. It is the game that matters. It is enough, says the novelist whom I enjoy above all other novelists, that an honourable man has reported these sensible extravagancies without desire to enter on them afresh. But it is not enough, never enough, to desist from experiment until the purpose of experiment has been achieved. The search for the right renewal of the game of chess is a long one. De Quincey has a phrase about " the infinite regressus of the phoenix." The phoenix is immortal; so is the mutual happiness which can be found at chess; if not through these little inventions, then through some other.*

I am now, as Polybius would say, at the end of my quest. But it was at such periods, I've noticed, that Polybius allowed himself a coda.

Within a year of Mr. Bird's proposed modification for the game of chess (and this is my last wave to Old Bird, as he recedes, along with Manetho) a light opera called *Trial by Jury* was presented to the world by a couple of gallant amateurs named Gilbert and Sullivan. There was a chorus much beloved by Doctors (and a wave to him too) which ran:

> Consider the moral I pray,
> Nor bring a young fellow to sorrow,
> Who loves this young lady to-day,
> And loves that young lady to-morrow.

Madame Doctors loved to hear Doctors sing that — not without a delicious apprehension — no woman born of woman had less cause to fear any husband's

* I cannot resist one final footnote, as I hand over these proofs and climb aboard the *Queen Mary*. It is another message from Lasker's great friend, Harold M. Phillips:

"Referring to the corridor, please to note that if the rule is made that the King may not find *sanctuary* in the corridor that also means that a King may not personally *invade* the corridor, so that a King and Rook's Pawn against the King will therefore not win in the same position as they would not win on the old board.

I am just thinking that you had better let me know every day where you are in Europe so that I can telephone you long distance if a new thought occurs to me, — not about business or even politics or matters of international policy or even a possible discovery of a manuscript in the handwriting of Shakespeare, but about the corridor!

H. M. P."

declension — yet (and I salute her gallant memory) she *was* jealous of Miss Mathematics. So far as I'm concerned, I think I can withstand the easy changeability as considered above by Gilbert. I don't even feel too desperately about the vanishing of Simpson's Chess Divan. It's not the changes in themselves, or even the losses in themselves, that count so much as the intent. The intent is, the improvement of the game. Four hundred years of study of the square board, and the increasing crystallization resulting from that study, seem to call for a change in chess, maybe later, maybe now. Another four centuries, or forty, may call for other changes. Not changes merely to reverse the balance, to permit the ignorant, the grasshopper instead of the ant, to win. " No," cries the great Lasker in his *Manual of Chess*. " Into a win? No, this proportion is not the right one. Into initiative, into a promising game. . . ." Into a game that comes alive, that is shared by both players, and shared fairly.

PENDANT

To find out the right procedure for the Knight's tour around the corridor board, I follow Euler's method. Euler begins, on any board, by moving the Knight at random until it has no further move open to it. With care this will leave only a few squares untraversed. Then Euler establishes certain rules by which these vacant squares can be interpolated into various parts of the circuit; also, by which the tour can be made re-entrant, so that not only does the Knight land upon every square, but also returns to his starting-place.

One may start anywhere, but I feel the most pleasant opening is from the Knight's traditional position. Thus Figure 11 shows a corridor board with a Knight's square numbered as 1. I begin his tour around the board, in which he is to visit every square but each square only once, by moving him at random, yet so as to fill

	11	22	9	26	69	66	29	32	
23	8	25	68	65	28	33	46	43	30
12	21	10	27	70	67	**B**	31	34	45
7	24	13	20	**A**	64	71	44	47	42
14	19	16	57	72	**C**	48	41	52	35
17	6	3	60	63	58	55	38	49	40
2	15	18	5	56	61	**D**	53	36	51
	4	1	62	59	54	37	50	39	

FIGURE 11

the first three files as soon as possible. Of course there are alternatives; but following this particular figure, the first 25 moves are used to exhaust the three left-hand files with only three moves

(5, 9, 20) into the fourth file. Then as the Knight prances across the top rows he achieves a symmetrical position, the square numbered 29 being vis-a-vis square 1. From square 29 another 25 moves will exhaust the three right-hand files with three moves (33, 37, 48) into the fourth file from the right. That brings the Knight to square 53.

Now, instead of striving to fill in the center completely, which would require a masterly guess, it is just as effective, and much easier, to achieve an arrangement such as shown in Figure 11, where several squares (in this case the four squares named A, B, C, D) remain unvisited, but — which is the important fact — are themselves connectible by Knight's moves.

In effect, Figure 11 shows the corridor board covered by two Knight's tours, the major one being the route from 1 to 72, the minor one being the route A, B, C, D. Neither of these routes are re-entrant. Euler's next step is to make the route from 1 to 72 re-entrant — that is, to make it a closed circuit — and the final step will be to interpolate the minor route A, B, C, D into that circuit.

To make the route from 1 to 72 re-entrant, you notice that square 1 commands squares 2, 6, 60, and that among the squares commanded by square 72 are the three squares 3, 5, 61. One of Euler's observations was that a tour can always be made re-entrant if the squares commanded by the end positions differ in their numbering by unity. Here we have just seen that among the squares commanded by the end positions there are three pairs which differ by unity; namely, 2 and 3; 6 and 5; 60 and 61. It is immaterial which pair we use.

Suppose we select the pair 6 and 5. Then, to improve on Figure 11, what we want to do is to reverse the numbering of the route from 6 to 72. That will send the Knight around that part of the major route in the reverse direction. So in Figure 11 you proceed to replace the numbers 72, 71, . . . 7, 6 by the numbers 6, 7, . . . 71, 72; and the result of that is shown in Figure 12.

In Figure 12 the route from 1 to 72 is re-entrant, and it only remains to interpolate into that closed circuit the four squares A, B, C, D.

In this particular case the interpolation is extremely simple. In

FIGURE 12

the minor circuit the Knight may pass from A to D or vice versa
by Knight's moves. Inspection of the figure shows that D commands the square 19 and A commands the square 20, so that the
steps D, C, B, A, taken in that direction, fall right into the route
of Figure 12 between squares 19 and 20. Thus all that is needed
is to give to the squares D, C, B, A the numbers 20, 21, 22, 23
respectively, and to renumber as 24 the square hitherto numbered
as 20, and for all of the other numbers in Figure 12 greater than
20, to make a corresponding addition of 4. This results in a final
figure, already given on page 103 as Figure 8, which shows a
complete re-entrant path for the Knight's tour on the corridor
board.

The analysis for the re-entrant tour of Figure 9 in the text is
similar, and presents no difficulty.

DEDICATION

Herein Diggon Davie is devised to be a shepheard, that in hope of more gayne, drove his sheepe into a farre countrye. . . .

Spenser, *The Shepheardes Calender* (*September*)

AT the end of this odd tour around the chessboard I think less harshly of my brother Christopher than I did at the beginning. He got me into it, and now another eminent pixie comes to rescue me from·the embarrassment of how to get it published. As Edmund Spenser is the poet's poet, so in our time Ben Huebsch is the publisher's publisher. For twenty years the world has been the poorer for the disappearance of the imprint " B. W. Huebsch." For twenty years the world has missed his traditional candlestick. Christopher put that brave statement on the title-page: " Le jeu vaut la chandelle." I am not so sure about that, but that Ben should permit it, and that he should revive his imprint for the one purpose of producing this animula, is a compliment which I deeply respect.

Perhaps the little thing should be dedicated to Kit and Ben. But (much as I love them) it isn't. No, it has to be understood that this is one of the products of The Both-Ends Candle-Burning Company (a subsidiary of The Midnight Oil Corporation) and by contract all such products are dedicated gently and simply to one member of my own, and to four members of a younger, generation. If in recent times I should have been able to have more of their companionship I shouldn't have bothered with the lesser pleasures of attempting to write something which is only

> . . . like to something I remember,
> A great while since, a long, long time ago.